Retire 1
Planning for a Comfortable and Secure Retirement

Retire Rich
Planning for a Comfortable and Secure Retirement

By

Maxwell Sterling

Vij Books
New Delhi (India)

Published by

Vij Books
(Publishers, Distributors & Importers)
4836/24, 3rd Floor, Ansari Road
Delhi – 110 002
Phone: 91-11-43596460
Mobile: 98110 94883
e-mail: contact@vijpublishing.com
www.vijbooks.in

ISBN: 978-81-19438-40-2 (PB)

Contents

Introduction to Retirement Planning

Retirement is a significant milestone in life, representing the culmination of years of hard work and dedication. It is a time to relax, pursue passions, and enjoy the fruits of labor. However, achieving a comfortable and secure retirement requires careful planning and foresight. This book serves as your comprehensive guide to retirement planning, offering insights, strategies, and practical advice to help you navigate this important phase of life with confidence and peace of mind. The book elaborates on the relevant topics as enumerated below.

Understanding Retirement

Retirement is more than just a date on a calendar; it is a life transition that involves a shift in roles, routines, and priorities. Many people approach retirement with a mix of excitement and apprehension, unsure of what to expect or how to prepare. In this chapter, we will explore the various aspects of retirement, including the emotional, psychological, and financial aspects. We will also debunk common myths and misconceptions about retirement, helping you to approach this phase of life with a clear and realistic mindset.

The Importance of Retirement Planning

Retirement planning is essential for ensuring a smooth transition into retirement. It involves setting goals, creating a budget, and making informed decisions about savings and investments. Proper planning can help you avoid financial hardships in retirement and ensure that you have enough resources to maintain your desired lifestyle. In this chapter, we will discuss the importance of retirement planning and its long-term benefits.

Setting Retirement Goals

Setting clear and achievable goals is the foundation of a successful retirement plan. In this chapter, we will discuss how to identify your retirement goals, taking into account your lifestyle preferences, financial obligations, and aspirations. We will also explore strategies for setting realistic goals and adjusting them as your circumstances change.

Creating a Retirement Budget

A retirement budget is a crucial tool for managing your finances in retirement. It helps you track your income and expenses, identify areas where you can save money, and ensure that you can maintain your desired standard of living. In this chapter, we will discuss how to create a retirement budget that aligns with your goals and lifestyle, taking into account factors such as inflation, healthcare costs, and unexpected expenses.

Managing Debt Before Retirement

Debt can be a significant burden in retirement, eating into your savings and limiting your financial freedom. In this chapter, we will discuss strategies for managing and reducing debt before retirement, including consolidating loans, negotiating lower interest rates, and prioritizing high-interest debt.

Understanding Retirement Accounts

Retirement accounts, such as 401(k) plans and IRAs, play a crucial role in retirement planning. In this chapter, we will discuss the different types of retirement accounts available, their tax implications, and how to maximize their benefits. We will also explore strategies for diversifying your retirement portfolio and managing risk.

Investment Strategies for Retirement

Investing is a key component of retirement planning, helping you grow your savings and generate income in retirement. In this chapter, we will discuss different investment strategies for retirement, including stocks, bonds, real estate, and alternative investments. We will also explore the importance of diversification and asset allocation in managing risk and achieving long-term growth.

Income Sources in Retirement

In retirement, you will rely on various sources of income to meet your financial needs. In this chapter, we will discuss the different sources of retirement income, including Social Security, pensions, annuities, and withdrawals from retirement accounts. We will also explore strategies for maximizing your income and managing withdrawals to minimize taxes and maximize benefits.

Healthcare and Insurance in Retirement

Healthcare costs can be a significant expense in retirement, so it's essential to plan for them carefully. In this chapter, we will discuss Medicare, Medicaid, long-term care insurance, and other healthcare options available to retirees. We will also explore strategies for managing healthcare costs and ensuring that you have adequate coverage in retirement.

Estate Planning

Estate planning is an essential part of retirement planning, helping you protect your assets and ensure that your wishes are carried out after your passing. In this chapter, we will discuss wills, trusts, beneficiary designations, and other estate planning tools that can help you plan for the future and protect your loved ones.

Lifestyle Considerations in Retirement

Retirement is not just about finances; it's also about lifestyle. In this chapter, we will discuss how to plan for your ideal retirement lifestyle, including where to live, how to stay active and engaged, and how to pursue your passions and interests in retirement.

Managing Risks in Retirement

Retirement comes with its share of risks, including inflation, market volatility, and longevity. In this chapter, we will discuss strategies for managing these risks, including diversification, asset allocation, and insurance.

Preparing for Unexpected Events

Unexpected events, such as a major illness or natural disaster, can derail your retirement plans. In this chapter, we will discuss strategies for preparing for and coping with unexpected events, including building an emergency fund and having a backup plan in place.

Monitoring and Adjusting Your Retirement Plan

Retirement planning is an ongoing process that requires regular monitoring and adjustments. In this chapter, we will discuss how to review your retirement plan regularly, make necessary adjustments, and stay on track to meet your goals.

Conclusion: Enjoying a Secure and Fulfilling Retirement

In conclusion, retirement planning is a critical process that requires careful consideration and proactive decision-making. By following the advice and strategies outlined in this book, you can create a retirement plan that will help you achieve financial security and peace of mind in retirement. Remember, retirement is not the end of the road but the beginning of a new chapter in your life. Embrace it with confidence and optimism, knowing that you have taken the necessary steps to retire rich and live the life you deserve.

Understanding Retirement

Retirement is a significant life transition that marks the end of a person's career and the beginning of a new phase of life. It is a time when individuals leave the workforce, typically in their 60s or 70s, and begin to rely on their accumulated savings and investments for income. Retirement can be a time of great joy and freedom, but it can also be a source of anxiety and uncertainty if not planned for properly.

Transition and Change

Retirement is not just a financial event but also an emotional and psychological one. For many people, their identity and sense of purpose are closely tied to their work. Retirement can therefore bring about feelings of loss, as individuals adjust to a new routine and a different way of life. It can also be a time of excitement and anticipation, as retirees look forward to pursuing hobbies, traveling, and spending more time with family and friends.

Financial Considerations

One of the key aspects of retirement planning is ensuring that you have enough money to support yourself throughout your retirement years. This requires careful planning and saving during your working years. Factors such as inflation, healthcare costs, and life expectancy need to be taken into account when determining how much money you will need in retirement.

Social Security and Pensions

Social Security and pensions are two common sources of retirement income. Social Security is a government program that provides a monthly income to eligible retirees, based on their earnings history. Pensions are retirement plans offered by some employers, which pay a monthly income to retirees based on their years of service and salary.

Healthcare Considerations

Healthcare is another important consideration in retirement planning. As people age, their healthcare needs tend to increase, so it's important to have a plan in place to cover these costs. Medicare is a federal health insurance program that provides coverage to eligible retirees, but it does not cover all healthcare expenses. Long-term care insurance is another option for covering healthcare costs in retirement.

Lifestyle Changes

Retirement often brings about changes in lifestyle. Many retirees choose to downsize their homes, travel more, or pursue hobbies and interests that they did not have time for during their working years. It's important to plan for these lifestyle changes and adjust your budget accordingly.

Emotional and Psychological Aspects

Retirement can be a time of mixed emotions. While many people look forward to retirement as a time to relax and enjoy life, others may struggle with feelings of boredom, isolation, or a loss of purpose. It's important to plan for these emotional and psychological aspects of retirement and find ways to stay engaged and fulfilled during this phase of life.

Conclusion

In conclusion, retirement is a major life transition that requires careful planning and consideration. By understanding the financial, social, and emotional aspects of retirement, you can better prepare yourself for this new chapter in your life. Whether you're just starting to plan for retirement or are already retired, it's never too late to take control of your financial future and ensure a comfortable and secure retirement.

The Importance of Retirement Planning

Retirement is a significant milestone in life, representing the culmination of years of hard work and dedication. It's a time to relax, pursue passions, and enjoy the fruits of labor. However, achieving a comfortable and secure retirement requires careful planning and foresight. This is where retirement planning plays a crucial role.

Financial Security

One of the primary reasons retirement planning is essential is to ensure financial security in retirement. Without proper planning, retirees may find themselves struggling to make ends meet, unable to afford basic necessities or unexpected expenses. Retirement planning helps individuals determine how much money they will need in retirement and develop a strategy to achieve that goal.

Setting Realistic Goals

Retirement planning also helps individuals set realistic goals for their retirement years. Whether it's traveling the world, pursuing a hobby, or simply relaxing at home, having clear goals can provide a sense of direction and purpose in retirement. By planning ahead, individuals can make informed decisions about how to allocate their resources to achieve their goals.

Managing Debt

Another important aspect of retirement planning is managing debt. Carrying debt into retirement can significantly impact a retiree's financial security, as debt payments can eat into retirement savings. Retirement planning helps individuals develop a strategy for paying off debt before retirement, ensuring a more comfortable financial situation in retirement.

Maximizing Savings and Investments

Retirement planning also involves maximizing savings and investments to build a nest egg for retirement. This includes contributing to retirement accounts such as 401(k)s and IRAs, as well as investing wisely to generate returns. By starting early and consistently saving and investing, individuals can take advantage of compound interest and grow their retirement savings over time.

Minimizing Taxes

Retirement planning can also help individuals minimize taxes in retirement. By understanding the tax implications of different retirement accounts and investment strategies, individuals can develop a tax-efficient retirement plan that maximizes their after-tax income in retirement.

Healthcare Costs

Healthcare costs are a significant expense in retirement, and retirement planning can help individuals prepare for these costs. By understanding Medicare and other healthcare options available in retirement, individuals can develop a plan to cover healthcare expenses and ensure access to quality care.

Legacy Planning

Retirement planning also involves legacy planning, or planning for how assets will be distributed after death. By developing an estate plan, individuals can ensure that their assets are distributed according to their wishes and minimize estate taxes for their heirs.

Peace of Mind

Perhaps most importantly, retirement planning provides peace of mind. Knowing that you have a plan in place for your retirement years can reduce stress and anxiety about the future. It allows individuals to retire with confidence, knowing that they have taken the necessary steps to ensure a comfortable and secure retirement.

In conclusion, retirement planning is essential for achieving financial security, setting realistic goals, managing debt, maximizing savings and investments, minimizing taxes, preparing for healthcare costs, planning for legacy, and providing peace of mind. Whether you're just starting to plan for retirement or are already retired, it's never too late to take control of your financial future and ensure a comfortable and secure retirement.

Setting Retirement Goals

Retirement is a time of transition, a new chapter in life where you have the opportunity to pursue your passions, explore new interests, and enjoy the freedom that comes with financial independence. Setting retirement goals is an important step in planning for this phase of life, as it helps you define what you want to achieve and how you will get there. In this chapter, we will explore the importance of setting retirement goals, the types of goals you may want to consider, and strategies for achieving them.

The Importance of Setting Retirement Goals

Setting retirement goals is crucial for several reasons. First and foremost, it helps you envision your ideal retirement lifestyle. By defining what you want your retirement to look like, you can begin to make the necessary plans and preparations to turn that vision into reality.

Setting retirement goals also helps you prioritize your financial resources. Retirement often comes with a fixed income, so it's essential to prioritize your spending and savings to ensure that you can afford the things that are most important to you in retirement.

Additionally, setting retirement goals can give you a sense of purpose and direction in retirement. Having goals to work towards can help you stay motivated and engaged, leading to a more fulfilling retirement experience.

Types of Retirement Goals

Retirement goals can be broadly categorized into three main types: financial goals, lifestyle goals, and personal development goals.

Financial Goals

Financial goals are related to your finances and include things like:

> ➢ Saving a certain amount of money for retirement
>
> ➢ Paying off debt before retirement
>
> ➢ Maintaining a certain standard of living in retirement
>
> ➢ Leaving a financial legacy for your loved ones

Lifestyle Goals

Lifestyle goals are related to how you want to spend your time in retirement and include things like:

> ➢ Traveling to new places
>
> ➢ Pursuing hobbies and interests
>
> ➢ Volunteering or giving back to the community
>
> ➢ Spending time with family and friends

Personal Development Goals

Personal development goals are related to your personal growth and well-being and include things like:

> ➢ Staying healthy and active in retirement

> ➤ Learning new skills or taking up new hobbies

> ➤ Finding purpose and meaning in retirement

> ➤ Maintaining a sense of independence and autonomy

Strategies for Achieving Retirement Goals

Once you have identified your retirement goals, the next step is to develop a plan for achieving them. Here are some strategies to help you achieve your retirement goals:

1. Start Early

One of the most effective strategies for achieving retirement goals is to start saving and planning early. The earlier you start saving for retirement, the more time your money has to grow through compounding.

2. Set Specific, Measurable Goals

When setting retirement goals, it's essential to make them specific and measurable. For example, instead of saying, "I want to travel more in retirement," you could say, "I want to take one international trip per year in retirement." This makes it easier to track your progress and adjust your plans as needed.

3. Create a Budget

Creating a budget is an essential step in achieving your retirement goals. A budget can help you track your income and expenses, identify areas where you can save money, and ensure that you are living within your means.

4. Maximize Retirement Savings

Maximizing your retirement savings is crucial for achieving your financial goals in retirement. Take advantage of employer-sponsored retirement plans, such as 401(k)s, and consider contributing to an individual retirement account (IRA) to supplement your savings.

5. Diversify Your Investments

Diversifying your investments can help you manage risk and achieve better returns over time. Consider investing in a mix of stocks, bonds, and other assets to achieve a balanced portfolio.

6. Review and Adjust Your Goals Regularly

Lastly, it's essential to review and adjust your retirement goals regularly. Life circumstances can change, so it's important to revisit your goals periodically and make adjustments as needed.

In conclusion, setting retirement goals is a crucial step in planning for a comfortable and fulfilling retirement. By defining your goals, developing a plan, and taking action, you can work towards achieving the retirement of your dreams. Whether your goals are financial, lifestyle-related, or personal development-focused, setting clear and achievable goals can help you stay motivated and on track to achieve the retirement you envision.

Creating a Retirement Budget

Creating a retirement budget is a crucial step in planning for a comfortable and secure retirement. A retirement budget helps you determine how much money you will need in retirement, track your income and expenses, and ensure that you can maintain your desired standard of living throughout your retirement years. In this chapter, we will explore the importance of creating a retirement budget, how to create one, and tips for sticking to your budget.

Why Create a Retirement Budget?

A retirement budget is essential for several reasons. First and foremost, it helps you determine how much money you will need in retirement. By calculating your expected expenses and income in retirement, you can get a clear picture of whether you are on track to meet your financial goals.

Second, a retirement budget helps you track your spending and identify areas where you can save money. This can be especially important in retirement, when you may be living on a fixed income and need to make every dollar count.

Finally, a retirement budget can help you plan for unexpected expenses and emergencies. By setting aside money for emergencies and unexpected expenses, you can avoid dipping into your retirement savings and maintain your financial security.

How to Create a Retirement Budget

Creating a retirement budget involves several steps:

1.   Calculate Your Expected Expenses: Start by calculating your expected expenses in retirement. This includes essential expenses such as housing, food, transportation, healthcare, and insurance, as well as discretionary expenses such as travel, entertainment, and hobbies.

2.   Estimate Your Income: Next, estimate your income in retirement. This includes income from sources such as Social Security, pensions, retirement accounts, and any other sources of income you expect to have in retirement.

3.   Calculate the Shortfall or Surplus: Compare your expected expenses to your estimated income to determine if you will have a shortfall or surplus in retirement. If you have a shortfall, you may need to adjust your budget or consider ways to increase your income or reduce your expenses. If you have a surplus, you can decide how to allocate the extra money, such as saving more for future expenses or enjoying more discretionary spending.

4.   Review and Adjust Regularly: It's essential to review and adjust your retirement budget regularly. Life circumstances can change, so it's important to revisit your budget periodically and make adjustments as needed.

Tips for Sticking to Your Retirement Budget

Sticking to your retirement budget can be challenging, but with some discipline and planning, it is achievable. Here are some tips to help you stick to your retirement budget:

1.   Track Your Spending: Keep track of your expenses to ensure that you are staying within your budget. There are many apps and tools available that can help you track your spending and identify areas where you can cut back.

2.   Avoid Impulse Purchases: Before making a purchase, especially a significant one, take some time to consider whether it fits into your budget and is a necessary expense.

3.   Plan for Large Expenses: Plan ahead for large expenses such as home repairs or vehicle maintenance. Setting aside money for these expenses in advance can help you avoid going over budget.

4.   Be Flexible: Be willing to adjust your budget as needed. If you find that your expenses are higher than expected, look for ways to reduce costs in other areas to stay within your budget.

5.   Seek Professional Advice: If you are struggling to stick to your budget, consider seeking advice from a financial advisor. They can help you identify areas where you can save money and develop a plan to achieve your financial goals.

In conclusion, creating a retirement budget is an essential step in planning for a comfortable and secure retirement. By calculating your expected expenses, estimating your income, and tracking your spending, you can ensure that you are on track to meet your financial goals in retirement. Sticking to your budget may require some discipline and planning, but with careful management, you can enjoy a fulfilling retirement without financial stress.

Managing Debt Before Retirement

Managing debt before retirement is crucial for ensuring a smooth transition into this new phase of life. Carrying debt into retirement can significantly impact your financial security, as debt payments can eat into your retirement savings and limit your financial flexibility. In this chapter, we will explore strategies for managing and reducing debt before retirement, including consolidating loans, negotiating lower interest rates, and prioritizing high-interest debt.

1. Assess Your Debt

The first step in managing debt before retirement is to assess your current debt situation. Make a list of all your debts, including credit card debt, mortgage, car loans, and any other outstanding loans. Note the total amount owed, the interest rates, and the monthly payments.

2. Create a Debt Repayment Plan

Once you have a clear picture of your debt, create a debt repayment plan. Start by prioritizing your debts based on interest rates, with higher-interest debts being paid off first. Consider using the snowball or avalanche method to pay off your debts, depending on your preference and financial situation.

3. Consolidate Debt

If you have multiple high-interest debts, consider consolidating them into a single loan with a lower interest rate. Debt consolidation can simplify your payments and potentially save you money on interest charges. However, be sure to carefully review the terms and fees associated with the consolidation loan before proceeding.

4. Negotiate Lower Interest Rates

Another option for managing debt before retirement is to negotiate lower interest rates with your creditors. Contact your creditors directly and explain your situation. They may be willing to lower your interest rate, especially if you have a history of on-time payments.

5. Cut Expenses

To free up more money for debt repayment, consider cutting expenses where possible. Look for areas where you can reduce spending, such as dining out less frequently, canceling unused subscriptions, or finding cheaper alternatives for goods and services.

6. Increase Income

Increasing your income can also help you pay off debt more quickly. Consider taking on a part-time job, freelancing, or selling items you no longer need to generate extra income that can be put toward debt repayment.

7. Avoid Taking on New Debt

While you are working to pay off existing debt, it's important to avoid taking on new debt. Try to pay for purchases with cash or debit instead of using credit cards, and avoid financing new purchases unless absolutely necessary.

8. Seek Financial Advice

If you are struggling to manage your debt before retirement, consider seeking advice from a financial advisor. They can help you develop a personalized debt repayment plan and provide guidance on how to improve your financial situation.

In conclusion, managing debt before retirement is essential for ensuring a smooth transition into this new phase of life. By assessing your debt, creating a repayment plan, consolidating debt, negotiating lower interest rates, cutting expenses, increasing income, avoiding new debt, and seeking financial advice, you can take control of your debt and work toward a debt-free retirement.

Understanding Retirement Accounts

Retirement accounts play a crucial role in retirement planning, providing individuals with tax-advantaged ways to save for retirement. Understanding the different types of retirement accounts available can help you make informed decisions about how to save and invest for your retirement. In this chapter, we will explore the various types of retirement accounts, their features, benefits, and tax implications.

Types of Retirement Accounts

There are several types of retirement accounts available, each with its own features and benefits. Some of the most common types of retirement accounts include:

1.   401(k) Plans: 401(k) plans are employer-sponsored retirement plans that allow employees to contribute a portion of their salary to a retirement account on a pre-tax basis. Employers may also match a portion of the employee's contributions, providing additional savings.

2.   Traditional IRAs: Traditional IRAs are individual retirement accounts that allow individuals to contribute a certain amount of money each year on a pre-tax basis. Contributions to a traditional IRA may be tax-deductible, and taxes are deferred on investment earnings until withdrawals are made in retirement.

3.   Roth IRAs: Roth IRAs are similar to traditional IRAs, but contributions are made on an after-tax basis. Qualified withdrawals from a Roth IRA are tax-free, providing tax-free income in retirement.

4. **SEP IRAs**: SEP IRAs are Simplified Employee Pension IRAs that are available to self-employed individuals and small business owners. Contributions to a SEP IRA are tax-deductible, and taxes are deferred on investment earnings until withdrawals are made in retirement.

5. **SIMPLE IRAs**: SIMPLE IRAs are Savings Incentive Match Plan for Employees IRAs that are available to small businesses with fewer than 100 employees. Employees can contribute a portion of their salary to a SIMPLE IRA on a pre-tax basis, and employers are required to make either matching or non-elective contributions.

6. **403(b) Plans**: 403(b) plans are retirement plans available to employees of certain tax-exempt organizations, such as schools, hospitals, and churches. Contributions to a 403(b) plan are made on a pre-tax basis, and taxes are deferred on investment earnings until withdrawals are made in retirement.

7. **457(b) Plans**: 457(b) plans are retirement plans available to employees of state and local governments and certain non-profit organizations. Contributions to a 457(b) plan are made on a pre-tax basis, and taxes are deferred on investment earnings until withdrawals are made in retirement.

Benefits of Retirement Accounts

Retirement accounts offer several benefits to individuals planning for retirement, including:

1.   Tax Advantages: Contributions to retirement accounts are often tax-deductible, and taxes on investment earnings are deferred until withdrawals are made in retirement. This

can help individuals reduce their current tax liability and grow their retirement savings more quickly.

2.   Employer Contributions: Many employer-sponsored retirement plans, such as 401(k) plans, offer employer matching contributions, providing employees with additional savings for retirement.

3.   Investment Options: Retirement accounts offer a wide range of investment options, allowing individuals to choose investments that align with their risk tolerance and investment goals.

4.   Asset Protection: Retirement accounts are often protected from creditors in the event of bankruptcy or other financial difficulties, providing added security for retirement savings.

Considerations for Choosing a Retirement Account

When choosing a retirement account, there are several factors to consider, including:

1.   Employer Match: If your employer offers a matching contribution to a retirement account, it's often beneficial to contribute enough to receive the full match, as it is essentially free money.

2.   Tax Considerations: Consider whether you prefer to receive a tax deduction for contributions now (traditional IRA or 401(k)) or have tax-free withdrawals in retirement (Roth IRA).

3.   Investment Options: Look for retirement accounts that offer a range of investment options that align with your investment goals and risk tolerance.

4.   Fees: Consider the fees associated with the retirement account, including administrative fees, investment fees, and any other fees that may apply.

5.   Withdrawal Rules: Be aware of the withdrawal rules for the retirement account, including any penalties for early withdrawal before age 59 1/2.

In conclusion, understanding retirement accounts is essential for making informed decisions about how to save and invest for retirement. By familiarizing yourself with the different types of retirement accounts available, their features, benefits, and tax implications, you can develop a retirement savings strategy that aligns with your financial goals and helps you achieve a comfortable and secure retirement.

Investment Strategies for Retirement

Investing wisely is crucial for building a retirement nest egg that can support you throughout your golden years. Retirement planning requires a different approach to investing than other financial goals, as you need to balance growth with stability to ensure your savings last as long as you need them. In this chapter, we will explore various investment strategies for retirement, including asset allocation, diversification, and risk management.

1. Asset Allocation

Asset allocation is a key component of any retirement investment strategy. It involves dividing your investment portfolio among different asset classes, such as stocks, bonds, and cash equivalents, to achieve a balance of risk and return that aligns with your retirement goals and risk tolerance.

> **Stocks**: Stocks have historically provided the highest returns over the long term but also come with the highest level of risk. They are more volatile than other asset classes and can experience significant fluctuations in value. However, stocks also have the potential for significant growth, making them an important component of a retirement investment portfolio, especially for younger investors with a longer time horizon.

> **Bonds**: Bonds are generally considered less risky than stocks but offer lower returns. They provide a

steady stream of income through interest payments and are less volatile than stocks, making them a more conservative investment option for retirees or those approaching retirement.

> **Cash Equivalents**: Cash equivalents, such as money market funds and certificates of deposit (CDs), are the least risky type of investment but offer the lowest returns. They are suitable for short-term savings goals or as a place to park cash that you may need in the near future.

2. Diversification

Diversification is another essential component of a retirement investment strategy. It involves spreading your investments across different asset classes, industries, and geographic regions to reduce the impact of market volatility and minimize risk. Diversification can help protect your portfolio from significant losses if one investment performs poorly.

3. Risk Management

Risk management is critical when investing for retirement. While it's essential to seek growth to build your retirement savings, it's also crucial to protect your savings from significant losses. Here are some strategies for managing risk in your retirement portfolio:

> Asset Allocation: As mentioned earlier, asset allocation is a key risk management strategy. By diversifying your investments across different asset classes, you can reduce the impact of market volatility on your portfolio.

➢ Rebalancing: Rebalancing involves periodically adjusting your portfolio to maintain your desired asset allocation. For example, if stocks have performed well and now make up a larger percentage of your portfolio than you intended, you may need to sell some stocks and buy more bonds to rebalance your portfolio.

➢ Dollar-Cost Averaging: Dollar-cost averaging is a strategy where you invest a fixed amount of money at regular intervals, regardless of market conditions. This can help reduce the impact of market volatility on your investments and potentially lower your average cost per share over time.

➢ Avoiding Market Timing: Trying to time the market by buying and selling investments based on short-term market trends is generally not a successful strategy. Instead, focus on your long-term investment goals and stick to your investment plan.

4. Tax-Efficient Investing

Tax-efficient investing is another important consideration for retirement planning. By investing in tax-efficient ways, you can minimize the impact of taxes on your investment returns and potentially increase your after-tax income in retirement. Some tax-efficient investment strategies include:

➢ Utilizing Retirement Accounts: Contributing to tax-advantaged retirement accounts, such as 401(k)s and IRAs, can help you defer taxes on your investment earnings until retirement.

➢ Tax-Loss Harvesting: Tax-loss harvesting involves selling investments that have experienced a loss to offset gains in other investments, thereby reducing your tax liability.

➤ Choosing Tax-Efficient Investments: Some investments are more tax-efficient than others. For example, index funds and ETFs tend to be more tax-efficient than actively managed mutual funds due to lower turnover and capital gains distributions.

5. Long-Term Perspective

Finally, it's essential to maintain a long-term perspective when investing for retirement. While market fluctuations can be unsettling, it's important to remember that investing is a long-term endeavor. By staying invested and sticking to your investment plan, you can weather short-term market volatility and potentially achieve your long-term retirement goals.

In conclusion, investing for retirement requires a careful balance of growth and stability. By diversifying your investments, managing risk, investing tax-efficiently, and maintaining a long-term perspective, you can build a retirement portfolio that provides the income and security you need to enjoy a comfortable retirement.

Types of Retirement Investments

When planning for retirement, it's important to consider a variety of investment options to build a diversified portfolio that can help you achieve your financial goals. Here are some common types of retirement investments to consider:

1. Stocks

Stocks represent ownership in a company and can offer the potential for high returns over the long term. However, they also come with a higher level of risk compared to other investments, as stock prices can be volatile. Investing in individual stocks requires careful research and monitoring, but you can also invest in stocks through mutual funds or exchange-traded funds (ETFs) for a more diversified approach.

2. Bonds

Bonds are debt securities issued by governments, municipalities, or corporations to raise capital. Bonds typically pay periodic interest payments and return the principal investment at maturity. Bonds are generally considered less risky than stocks but offer lower potential returns. They can provide a stable source of income and help diversify a retirement portfolio.

3. Real Estate

Investing in real estate can provide a source of passive income and potential appreciation in property value. You can invest in real estate directly by purchasing rental properties or indirectly through real estate investment trusts (REITs) or real estate crowdfunding platforms. Real estate investments can offer a hedge against inflation and diversify your portfolio, but they also come with risks such as property maintenance costs and market fluctuations.

4. Mutual Funds

Mutual funds pool money from multiple investors to invest in a diversified portfolio of stocks, bonds, or other securities. Mutual funds are managed by professional fund managers, who make investment decisions on behalf of investors. Mutual funds offer diversification and professional management, but they also come with fees and expenses that can impact returns.

5. Exchange-Traded Funds (ETFs)

ETFs are similar to mutual funds but trade on stock exchanges like individual stocks. ETFs offer the diversification of mutual funds with the flexibility of trading like stocks. They typically have lower expense ratios than mutual funds and can be a cost-effective way to invest in a diversified portfolio of securities.

6. Retirement Accounts

Retirement accounts such as 401(k)s, IRAs, and Roth IRAs offer tax advantages that can help you save for retirement. Contributions to traditional 401(k)s and IRAs are made on a pre-tax basis, reducing your taxable income in the year of contribution. Withdrawals from these accounts are taxed as ordinary income. Roth 401(k)s and Roth IRAs, on the other hand, are funded with after-tax contributions, but qualified withdrawals are tax-free. These accounts can provide a tax-efficient way to save for retirement and grow your investments over time.

7. Annuities

Annuities are insurance products that provide a guaranteed income stream in retirement. There are several types of annuities, including immediate annuities, which provide income right away, and deferred annuities, which provide income at a later date. Annuities can provide a source of guaranteed income in retirement, but they often come with fees and restrictions that can impact returns.

8. Cash and Cash Equivalents

Cash and cash equivalents, such as savings accounts, certificates of deposit (CDs), and money market funds, provide a low-risk investment option for retirement savings. While they offer lower returns compared to stocks and bonds, they can provide stability and liquidity, making them suitable for short-term savings goals or as a source of emergency funds.

In conclusion, there are many types of retirement investments to consider when planning for retirement. By diversifying your investments across different asset classes and investment vehicles, you can build a retirement portfolio that meets your financial goals and risk tolerance. It's important to carefully research your investment options and consult with a financial advisor to develop a retirement investment strategy that is tailored to your individual needs and circumstances.

Risk Management in Retirement Investments

Managing risk is crucial when investing for retirement, as you want to protect your savings while still achieving your financial goals. Here are some key strategies for managing risk in retirement investments:

1. Asset Allocation

Asset allocation is the process of dividing your investment portfolio among different asset classes, such as stocks, bonds, and cash equivalents, to achieve a balance of risk and return that aligns with your investment goals and risk tolerance. A well-diversified portfolio can help reduce the impact of market volatility and minimize risk.

2. Diversification

Diversification involves spreading your investments across different asset classes, industries, and geographic regions to reduce the risk of loss from any single investment. By diversifying your portfolio, you can help protect against the impact of poor performance in one area of the market.

3. Rebalancing

Rebalancing involves periodically adjusting your portfolio to maintain your desired asset allocation. For example, if stocks have outperformed bonds and now make up a larger percentage of your portfolio than you intended, you may need to sell some stocks and buy more bonds to rebalance your portfolio. Rebalancing can help you stay on track with your investment goals and manage risk.

4. Risk Tolerance

Understanding your risk tolerance is important when investing for retirement. Your risk tolerance is the amount of risk you are willing and able to take with your investments. It's important to align your investment strategy with your risk tolerance to avoid taking on too much risk or too little risk.

5. Time Horizon

Your time horizon, or the number of years you have until you plan to retire, is another important factor to consider when managing risk in retirement investments. Generally, the longer your time horizon, the more risk you can afford to take with your investments, as you have more time to recover from any downturns in the market.

6. Investment Selection

Choosing the right investments is key to managing risk in retirement. Consider investments that offer a balance of risk and return, and avoid investments that are too risky or speculative. It's also important to regularly review your investments and make adjustments as needed based on changes in the market or your financial situation.

7. Emergency Fund

Having an emergency fund can help you manage risk in retirement by providing a source of funds to cover unexpected expenses or income disruptions. Aim to keep three to six months' worth of living expenses in a liquid, easily accessible account, such as a savings account or money market fund.

8. Professional Advice

Seeking advice from a financial advisor can help you develop a retirement investment strategy that is tailored to your individual needs and circumstances. A financial advisor can help you assess your risk tolerance, develop a diversified investment portfolio, and make informed decisions about managing risk in your retirement investments.

In conclusion, managing risk in retirement investments is essential for protecting your savings and achieving your financial goals. By diversifying your portfolio, rebalancing regularly, understanding your risk tolerance, and seeking professional advice, you can help ensure that your retirement investments are well-positioned to weather market volatility and provide you with a secure financial future.

Diversification and Asset Allocation in Retirement Investments

Diversification and asset allocation are two fundamental principles of investing that can help you manage risk and maximize returns in your retirement investments. Understanding these concepts and how to apply them to your investment strategy is crucial for building a portfolio that can help you achieve your long-term financial goals.

Diversification

Diversification involves spreading your investments across different asset classes, industries, and geographic regions to reduce the impact of market volatility and minimize the risk of loss from any single investment. By diversifying your portfolio, you can potentially improve your risk-adjusted returns and increase the likelihood of achieving your investment goals.

There are several ways to diversify your portfolio:

> ➢ Asset Classes: Invest in a mix of asset classes, such as stocks, bonds, and cash equivalents, to spread risk across different types of investments. Each asset class has its own risk and return characteristics, so diversifying across asset classes can help balance the risk and return of your portfolio.

> ➢ Individual Investments: Within each asset class, diversify your investments by investing in a variety of individual securities. For example, instead of investing in just one stock, invest in multiple stocks across different industries to reduce the risk of loss from any single company.

> ➢ Geographic Regions: Invest in companies or assets from different geographic regions to diversify your exposure to regional economic factors. This can help reduce the impact of economic downturns in any single region on your overall portfolio.

> ➢ Investment Vehicles: Diversify your investments across different types of investment vehicles, such as mutual funds, exchange-traded funds (ETFs), and individual securities. Each investment vehicle has its

own risk and return characteristics, so diversifying across different types of vehicles can help reduce risk.

Asset Allocation

Asset allocation is the process of dividing your investment portfolio among different asset classes based on your investment goals, risk tolerance, and time horizon. The goal of asset allocation is to create a balanced portfolio that can help you achieve your long-term financial goals while managing risk.

There are several factors to consider when determining your asset allocation:

> ➤ Investment Goals: Consider your investment goals, such as retirement, and how much risk you are willing to take to achieve those goals. Your asset allocation should align with your goals and risk tolerance.

> ➤ Risk Tolerance: Assess your risk tolerance, or the amount of risk you are willing and able to take with your investments. Your asset allocation should reflect your risk tolerance to avoid taking on too much or too little risk.

> ➤ Time Horizon: Consider your time horizon, or the number of years you have until you need to access your investments. A longer time horizon may allow you to take on more risk, while a shorter time horizon may require a more conservative approach.

> ➤ Diversification: Ensure that your asset allocation is well-diversified across different asset classes to

reduce the impact of market volatility and minimize risk.

In conclusion, diversification and asset allocation are essential principles of investing that can help you manage risk and maximize returns in your retirement investments. By diversifying your portfolio across different asset classes and using asset allocation to create a balanced portfolio, you can build a retirement portfolio that is well-positioned to achieve your long-term financial goals.

Income Sources in Retirement

Planning for retirement involves considering various income sources to ensure financial security and maintain your desired lifestyle. Understanding the different income sources available can help you create a comprehensive retirement income plan. Here are some common income sources in retirement:

1. Social Security

Social Security is a federal program that provides a monthly income to eligible retirees, as well as disabled individuals and survivors of deceased workers. The amount of your Social Security benefit is based on your earnings history and the age at which you begin receiving benefits. You can start receiving Social Security benefits as early as age 62, but your benefit amount will be reduced if you choose to start before your full retirement age (which is typically between 66 and 67, depending on your birth year). Delaying Social Security beyond your full retirement age can increase your benefit amount.

2. Pensions

Pensions are retirement plans offered by some employers that provide a monthly income to retirees. The amount of your pension benefit is typically based on your years of service and earnings history with the company. Some pensions offer a lump-sum payout option, while others provide a lifetime annuity. If you have a pension, it's important to understand the terms of your plan and how it will impact your retirement income.

3. Retirement Accounts (401(k), IRA, etc.)

Retirement accounts such as 401(k) plans and Individual Retirement Accounts (IRAs) are tax-advantaged accounts designed to help you save for retirement. These accounts allow you to contribute pre-tax or after-tax dollars, depending on the type of account, and earnings in the account grow tax-deferred. You can start withdrawing from these accounts penalty-free after age 59 1/2, and withdrawals are taxed as ordinary income. It's important to carefully consider your withdrawal strategy to minimize taxes and ensure your savings last throughout retirement.

4. Investment Income

Investment income from stocks, bonds, mutual funds, and other investments can provide a source of income in retirement. This income can come from dividends, interest payments, and capital gains. It's important to have a diversified investment portfolio to manage risk and maximize potential returns. Consider working with a financial advisor to develop an investment strategy that aligns with your retirement goals and risk tolerance.

5. Rental Income

If you own rental property, rental income can be a source of retirement income. Rental income can provide a steady stream of income in retirement, but it's important to consider the responsibilities and costs associated with being a landlord. You may also want to explore other real estate investment options, such as real estate investment trusts (REITs), which can provide exposure to real estate without the responsibilities of property ownership.

6. Part-Time Work

Some retirees choose to work part-time in retirement to supplement their income and stay active. Part-time work can provide additional income and social interaction, but it's important to consider how working may impact your retirement benefits, such as Social Security and pension payments. Be sure to understand the rules and limitations for earning income while receiving retirement benefits.

7. Annuities

Annuities are insurance products that provide a guaranteed income stream in retirement. There are several types of annuities, including immediate annuities, which provide income right away, and deferred annuities, which provide income at a later date. Annuities can provide a source of guaranteed income in retirement, but they often come with fees and restrictions that can impact returns. It's important to carefully consider the terms of an annuity and how it fits into your overall retirement income plan.

In conclusion, retirement income planning involves considering various income sources to ensure financial security and maintain your desired lifestyle. By understanding the different income sources available and how they work, you can create a comprehensive retirement income plan that meets your needs and goals.

Social Security Benefits in Retirement

Social Security is a federal program that provides retirement, disability, and survivor benefits to eligible individuals and their families. Understanding how Social Security benefits work and how they can impact your retirement income is important for planning your financial future.

1. Eligibility for Social Security Benefits

To be eligible for Social Security retirement benefits, you must have earned a certain number of work credits by paying Social Security taxes during your working years. The number of work credits required depends on your age at retirement, but most people need 40 credits (equivalent to about 10 years of work) to qualify for retirement benefits.

2. Determining Your Social Security Benefit Amount

Your Social Security retirement benefit amount is based on your earnings history and the age at which you choose to start receiving benefits. Your benefit is calculated using a formula that takes into account your highest 35 years of earnings, adjusted for inflation. The age at which you start receiving benefits also affects your benefit amount. You can start receiving Social Security retirement benefits as early as age 62, but your benefit amount will be reduced if you choose to start before your full retirement age (which is between 66 and 67, depending on your birth year). Delaying Social Security beyond your full retirement age can increase your benefit amount.

3. Types of Social Security Benefits

➤ Retirement Benefits: Retirement benefits are paid to eligible individuals who have reached the age of retirement and have enough work credits to qualify. The amount of your retirement benefit is based on your earnings history and the age at which you start receiving benefits.

➤ Spousal Benefits: Spousal benefits are paid to the spouses of eligible retirees. A spouse can receive up to 50% of the retiree's benefit amount, depending on their age and the age at which the retiree starts receiving benefits.

➤ Survivor Benefits: Survivor benefits are paid to the surviving spouses, children, and in some cases, parents of deceased workers who were eligible for Social Security benefits. The amount of survivor benefits depends on the worker's earnings history and the relationship of the survivor to the worker.

➤ Disability Benefits: Disability benefits are paid to eligible individuals who are unable to work due to a qualifying disability. To qualify for disability benefits, you must have a medical condition that is expected to last at least one year or result in death.

4. Impact of Working on Social Security Benefits

If you choose to work while receiving Social Security benefits, your benefits may be reduced if you earn more than a certain amount. This is known as the earnings limit. If you are under full retirement age for the entire year, Social Security will deduct $1 from your benefit payments for every $2 you earn above the annual limit ($19,560 in 2022). In the year you reach full retirement age, Social Security will deduct $1 for every $3 you earn above a different limit ($51,960 in 2022), but only counting earnings before the month you reach full retirement age.

5. Taxation of Social Security Benefits

Depending on your income, your Social Security benefits may be subject to federal income tax. If your combined income (adjusted gross income + nontaxable interest + half of your Social Security benefits) exceeds a certain threshold ($25,000 for individuals and $32,000 for married couples filing jointly), up to 85% of your Social Security benefits may be taxable.

In conclusion, Social Security benefits are an important source of income for many retirees. Understanding how Social Security benefits work and how they can impact your retirement income is essential for planning your financial future. By knowing your options and making informed decisions, you can maximize your Social Security benefits and enjoy a more secure retirement.

Pensions and Annuities in Retirement

Pensions and annuities are two types of retirement income that can provide a steady stream of income in retirement. Understanding how pensions and annuities work can help you make informed decisions about your retirement planning.

1. Pensions

Pensions are retirement plans offered by some employers that provide a guaranteed income stream to retirees. Pensions are typically based on your years of service with the company and your earnings history. The amount of your pension benefit is usually calculated using a formula that takes into account factors such as your salary and the number of years you worked for the company.

There are two main types of pensions:

> ➤ Defined Benefit Plans: With a defined benefit plan, your pension benefit is based on a specific formula, typically using factors such as your salary and years of service. The employer bears the investment risk and guarantees a specific benefit amount in retirement.

> ➤ Defined Contribution Plans: With a defined contribution plan, such as a 401(k) or 403(b) plan, you and/or your employer contribute to an individual account, and the value of the account depends on the contributions and investment performance. You are responsible for managing the investments in your account, and the income you receive in retirement depends on the value of your account at that time.

2. Annuities

Annuities are insurance products that provide a guaranteed income stream in retirement. Annuities are typically purchased from an insurance company using a lump sum payment or a series of payments. The insurance company then pays you a regular income stream, either for a specified period (such as a fixed number of years) or for life.

There are several types of annuities, including:

> ➤ Immediate Annuities: Immediate annuities start paying out income right away, usually within a year of purchase. They provide a guaranteed income stream for life or for a specified period.

> ➤ Deferred Annuities: Deferred annuities allow you to accumulate funds over time and then start receiving income at a later date. They can provide a guaranteed income stream in retirement and may offer tax-deferred growth on your investment.

> ➤ Fixed Annuities: Fixed annuities provide a fixed income stream based on a predetermined interest rate. They offer predictability and stability but may not keep pace with inflation.

> ➤ Variable Annuities: Variable annuities allow you to invest in a variety of sub-accounts, similar to mutual funds. The income you receive in retirement depends on the performance of your investments.

3. Considerations for Pensions and Annuities

When considering pensions and annuities for retirement income, it's important to weigh the following factors:

> ➤ Guaranteed Income: Pensions and some types of annuities provide a guaranteed income stream in retirement, which can help provide financial security.

> ➤ Inflation Protection: Some pensions and annuities may offer inflation protection, which can help ensure that your income keeps pace with rising prices.

> ➤ Tax Considerations: The tax treatment of pensions and annuities can vary depending on the type of plan and how the income is received. It's important to understand the tax implications before making a decision.

> ➤ Lump Sum vs. Annuity Payments: If you have a choice between taking a lump sum payment or receiving annuity payments, consider your financial goals, risk tolerance, and income needs in retirement.

In conclusion, pensions and annuities can be valuable sources of retirement income, providing a guaranteed income stream that can help you achieve financial security in retirement. It's important to understand how these options work and how they fit into your overall retirement plan. Consulting with a financial advisor can help you make informed decisions about pensions and annuities and create a retirement income strategy that meets your needs.

Withdrawal Strategies from Retirement Accounts

As you approach retirement, it's important to plan how you will withdraw money from your retirement accounts to ensure that your savings last throughout your retirement years. Here are some common withdrawal strategies from retirement accounts:

1. Required Minimum Distributions (RMDs)

Once you reach age 72 (70 ½ if you reached 70 ½ before January 1, 2020), you are generally required to start taking withdrawals from your traditional IRA, 401(k), and other retirement accounts. These withdrawals are known as Required Minimum Distributions (RMDs) and are calculated based on your account balance and life expectancy.

2. Systematic Withdrawal Plan

A systematic withdrawal plan involves withdrawing a set amount of money from your retirement account at regular intervals, such as monthly or annually. This can help you budget your retirement income and ensure a steady stream of income throughout retirement.

3. Withdrawals Based on Income Needs

Another approach is to withdraw money from your retirement accounts based on your income needs and financial goals. For example, you might withdraw more during years when you have higher expenses (such as travel or healthcare costs) and less during years when expenses are lower.

4. Withdrawals Based on Tax Considerations

You can also consider tax-efficient withdrawal strategies to minimize the tax impact of your withdrawals. For example, you might withdraw from taxable accounts first to allow tax-deferred accounts to continue growing, or you might strategically time withdrawals to stay within a lower tax bracket.

5. Bucket Strategy

The bucket strategy involves dividing your retirement savings into different "buckets" based on when you plan to use the money. For example, you might have a "cash bucket" for short-term expenses, a "bond bucket" for medium-term expenses, and a "stock bucket" for long-term growth. By matching your investments to your time horizon, you can manage risk and liquidity needs more effectively.

6. Withdrawals Based on Market Conditions

Some retirees adjust their withdrawal strategy based on market conditions. For example, if the stock market is performing well, they might withdraw more from their stock investments, and if the market is down, they might withdraw less or use other sources of income to avoid selling investments at a loss.

7. Annuity or Pension Payments

If you have purchased an annuity or have a pension, you may receive regular payments that can supplement your retirement income. These payments can provide a steady source of income in retirement and help you plan your withdrawals from other retirement accounts.

8. Consult with a Financial Advisor

It's important to consult with a financial advisor or tax professional to develop a withdrawal strategy that aligns with your financial goals, risk tolerance, and tax situation. A professional can help you navigate the complexities of retirement account withdrawals and make informed decisions about how to best manage your retirement savings.

Healthcare and Insurance in Retirement

Planning for healthcare and insurance needs is a critical aspect of retirement planning. As you age, healthcare expenses can increase, so it's important to understand your options for healthcare coverage and how to manage these costs in retirement.

1. Medicare

Medicare is a federal health insurance program for people age 65 and older, as well as some younger people with disabilities. Medicare has several parts that cover different services.

It's important to understand the coverage and costs associated with each part of Medicare and consider supplemental insurance, such as Medigap, to help cover out-of-pocket expenses not covered by Medicare.

2. Long-Term Care Insurance

Long-term care insurance can help cover the costs of long-term care services, such as nursing home care, assisted living, and in-home care. Long-term care can be expensive, and Medicare typically does not cover these costs, so long-term care insurance can help protect your assets and provide peace of mind.

3. Health Savings Accounts (HSAs)

HSAs are tax-advantaged accounts that can be used to pay for qualified medical expenses. Contributions to an HSA are tax-deductible, and withdrawals for qualified medical expenses are tax-free. HSAs can be a valuable tool for saving for healthcare expenses in retirement.

4. Retiree Health Benefits

Some employers offer retiree health benefits to their retirees, which can help cover healthcare costs not covered by Medicare. If you have retiree health benefits, be sure to understand the coverage and any costs associated with the plan.

5. Medicaid

Medicaid is a state and federal program that provides health coverage to low-income individuals and families. Medicaid covers a broad range of health services and can help cover healthcare costs in retirement for those who qualify.

6. Health and Wellness Expenses

In addition to insurance coverage, it's important to budget for health and wellness expenses in retirement, such as routine medical care, prescription medications, and other healthcare services. Staying healthy and active can help reduce healthcare costs and improve quality of life in retirement.

7. Review and Update Your Coverage Regularly

As your healthcare needs change in retirement, it's important to review and update your insurance coverage regularly to ensure it meets your needs. Consider working with a financial advisor or insurance agent who specializes in retirement planning to help you navigate your options and make informed decisions about healthcare and insurance coverage in retirement.

Medicare and Medicaid: Key Differences and Benefits

As you plan for retirement, understanding the basics of Medicare and Medicaid can be crucial for managing your healthcare needs and costs. Both programs are government-run, but they serve different populations and cover different services. Here's an overview of Medicare and Medicaid, including their key differences and benefits:

Medicare:

Medicare is a federal health insurance program primarily for people aged 65 and older, although it also covers some younger individuals with disabilities. Medicare has several parts, each covering different services:

> - Part A (Hospital Insurance): Covers inpatient hospital stays, skilled nursing facility care, hospice care, and some home health care services.

> - Part B (Medical Insurance): Covers outpatient care, doctor visits, preventive services, and some home health care services.

> - Part C (Medicare Advantage): Allows private insurance companies to provide Medicare benefits. These plans often include additional coverage, such as vision, dental, and prescription drug coverage.

> - Part D (Prescription Drug Coverage): Provides prescription drug coverage through private insurance companies that contract with Medicare.

Medicare is funded through payroll taxes and premiums paid by beneficiaries. Most people are automatically enrolled in Medicare Part A when they turn 65, but enrollment in Part B and other parts may require action on your part.

Medicaid:

Medicaid is a joint federal and state program that provides health coverage to low-income individuals and families. Eligibility and benefits vary by state, but Medicaid generally covers a broader range of services than Medicare, including long-term care, dental care, and mental health services.

Medicaid is funded jointly by the federal government and states, with states having flexibility in how they administer the program. Eligibility for Medicaid is based on income and other factors, and not all low-income individuals qualify for the program.

Key Differences:

1.   Population Served: Medicare primarily serves older adults aged 65 and older, as well as younger individuals with disabilities. Medicaid primarily serves low-income individuals and families of all ages.

2.   Coverage: Medicare covers a wide range of healthcare services for seniors, while Medicaid covers additional services and is more comprehensive in its coverage.

3.   Cost: Medicare beneficiaries may have to pay premiums, deductibles, and copayments for services, depending on the parts of Medicare they enroll in. Medicaid is generally free or low-cost for eligible individuals, with no or minimal out-of-pocket costs.

4.   Administration: Medicare is a federal program administered by the Centers for Medicare & Medicaid Services (CMS). Medicaid is a joint federal and state program, and states have flexibility in how they administer the program and set eligibility criteria.

Benefits:

Access to Healthcare: Both Medicare and Medicaid provide access to healthcare services for eligible individuals who may not otherwise be able to afford them.

1.   Financial Protection: Both programs can provide financial protection against high healthcare costs, although Medicaid provides more comprehensive coverage for low-income individuals.

2.   Long-Term Care: Medicaid covers long-term care services, such as nursing home care, which are not covered by Medicare.

In conclusion, Medicare and Medicaid are important programs that provide healthcare coverage to millions of Americans. Understanding the differences between the two programs can help you make informed decisions about your healthcare needs and coverage options in retirement.

Long-Term Care Insurance: Planning for Future Healthcare Needs

Long-term care (LTC) insurance is a type of insurance that helps cover the costs of long-term care services, such as nursing home care, assisted living, and in-home care. As you plan for retirement, considering long-term care insurance can be crucial for protecting your assets and ensuring that you receive the care you need in the future. Here's an overview of long-term care insurance, including how it works, what it covers, and factors to consider:

How Long-Term Care Insurance Works:

➢ Coverage: Long-term care insurance typically covers a range of long-term care services, including nursing home care, assisted living, adult day care, and in-home care. Some policies may also cover services such as home modifications and caregiver training.

➤ Benefit Amount: Long-term care insurance policies pay a daily or monthly benefit amount, up to a specified limit, to cover the costs of long-term care services. The benefit amount and coverage limits vary depending on the policy.

➤ Waiting Period: Most long-term care insurance policies have a waiting period, known as the elimination period, before benefits are paid. The length of the waiting period can vary, but it is typically 30, 60, or 90 days.

➤ Duration of Coverage: Long-term care insurance policies can provide coverage for a specified number of years (such as two, five, or ten years) or for the rest of your life, depending on the policy terms.

What Long-Term Care Insurance Covers:

➤ Nursing Home Care: Coverage for care in a skilled nursing facility, including room and board, nursing care, and therapy services.

➤ Assisted Living: Coverage for care in an assisted living facility, including assistance with activities of daily living (ADLs) such as bathing, dressing, and eating.

➤ In-Home Care: Coverage for home health care services, such as nursing care, physical therapy, and assistance with ADLs.

➤ Other Services: Some long-term care insurance policies may also cover other services, such as respite care, hospice care, and home modifications to accommodate disabilities.

Factors to Consider:

➤ Cost: Long-term care insurance premiums can vary widely depending on factors such as your age, health status, the amount of coverage, and the policy terms. It's important to compare quotes from different insurance companies and consider the long-term affordability of the premiums.

➤ Coverage Options: Some long-term care insurance policies offer additional features, such as inflation protection, which can help ensure that your benefits keep pace with rising healthcare costs. Consider whether these features are important to you when choosing a policy.

➤ Health Status: Your health status can affect your eligibility for long-term care insurance and the cost of premiums. It's important to apply for long-term care insurance while you are still healthy, as pre-existing conditions may affect your ability to qualify for coverage.

➤ Financial Considerations: Long-term care insurance can help protect your assets from the high costs of long-term care services. Consider how you will pay for long-term care if you do not have insurance coverage and how long-term care expenses could impact your retirement savings.

In conclusion, long-term care insurance can be an important part of your retirement planning strategy, providing financial protection against the high costs of long-term care services. It's important to carefully consider your options and choose a policy that meets your needs and budget. Working with a financial advisor can help you navigate the complexities of long-term care insurance and make informed decisions about your future healthcare needs.

Health Savings Accounts (HSAs): A Tax-Advantaged Tool for Healthcare Expenses

A Health Savings Account (HSA) is a tax-advantaged savings account that allows individuals with high-deductible health plans (HDHPs) to save for medical expenses. HSAs offer several benefits, including tax savings, flexibility, and the ability to save for future healthcare needs. Here's an overview of how HSAs work and how you can use them to manage your healthcare expenses:

How HSAs Work:

➢ Eligibility: To open and contribute to an HSA, you must be covered by a qualified HDHP and not be enrolled in Medicare. You cannot be claimed as a dependent on someone else's tax return.

➢ Contribution Limits: For 2022, the annual contribution limit for an individual with self-only coverage is $3,650, and for an individual with family coverage, it is $7,300. Individuals age 55 and older can make an additional "catch-up" contribution of $1,000 per year.

➢ Tax Advantages: Contributions to an HSA are tax-deductible, meaning you can deduct them from your taxable income, even if you do not itemize deductions. Withdrawals for qualified medical expenses are tax-free, making HSAs a tax-efficient way to save for healthcare expenses.

➢ Rollover: Unlike flexible spending accounts (FSAs), funds in an HSA roll over from year to year and are not forfeited if they are not used. This allows you to build a balance over time to cover future healthcare expenses.

Using an HSA:

➢ Qualified Medical Expenses: You can use HSA funds to pay for qualified medical expenses, including deductibles, copayments, coinsurance, and certain other expenses not covered by your HDHP. Qualified medical expenses are defined by the IRS and include a wide range of healthcare services and products.

➢ Non-Qualified Expenses: If you use HSA funds for non-qualified expenses before age 65, you will owe income tax on the withdrawal plus a 20% penalty. After age 65, you can use HSA funds for non-qualified expenses without penalty, but you will owe income tax on the withdrawal.

➢ Investment Options: Some HSAs offer investment options, allowing you to grow your savings over time. It's important to review the investment options and fees associated with your HSA to make informed investment decisions.

Benefits of HSAs:

> ➤ Tax Savings: Contributions to an HSA are tax-deductible, and withdrawals for qualified medical expenses are tax-free, providing a triple tax advantage.

> ➤ Flexibility: HSAs offer flexibility in how you use your funds, allowing you to pay for qualified medical expenses now or save for future healthcare needs.

> ➤ Portability: HSAs are portable, meaning you can take them with you if you change jobs or health insurance plans.

> ➤ Savings for Retirement: After age 65, you can use HSA funds for non-qualified expenses without penalty, providing a way to save for retirement healthcare expenses.

In conclusion, Health Savings Accounts (HSAs) are a valuable tool for managing healthcare expenses and saving for future medical needs. By taking advantage of the tax benefits and flexibility of HSAs, you can build a financial cushion for healthcare costs and improve your overall financial wellness.

Estate Planning: A Comprehensive Guide

Estate planning is the process of arranging for the transfer of your assets to your heirs or beneficiaries after your death, as well as planning for your own future financial and healthcare needs. A well-thought-out estate plan can help ensure that your assets are distributed according to your wishes, minimize taxes, and provide for your loved ones.

Key Components of Estate Planning:

1.   Will: A will is a legal document that outlines how you want your assets to be distributed after your death. It also allows you to name a guardian for any minor children and an executor to manage your estate.

2.   Trusts: A trust is a legal arrangement that allows a third party, known as the trustee, to hold assets on behalf of a beneficiary. Trusts can be used to manage assets during your lifetime and after your death, and can provide flexibility in how assets are distributed.

3.   Power of Attorney: A power of attorney is a legal document that gives someone else the authority to make financial or healthcare decisions on your behalf if you become incapacitated.

4.   Healthcare Directive: A healthcare directive, also known as a living will, is a legal document that outlines your wishes for medical treatment if you are unable to make decisions for yourself. It can also appoint someone to make healthcare decisions for you.

5.   Beneficiary Designations: Assets such as retirement accounts, life insurance policies, and bank accounts can be passed directly to beneficiaries by naming them as beneficiaries on the account. It's important to review and update beneficiary designations regularly to ensure they reflect your current wishes.

Benefits of Estate Planning:

1.   Control: Estate planning allows you to control how your assets are distributed after your death, ensuring that your wishes are carried out.

2.   Avoiding Probate: Proper estate planning can help your heirs avoid the time-consuming and expensive probate process, which is required to distribute assets according to state law if there is no will.

3.   Minimizing Taxes: Estate planning can help minimize estate taxes, which can be substantial for large estates. Strategies such as gifting, using trusts, and charitable giving can help reduce estate tax liability.

4.   Protecting Beneficiaries: Estate planning can help protect beneficiaries, especially minor children or those with special needs, by providing for their care and ensuring that assets are managed responsibly.

5.   Peace of Mind: Having an estate plan in place can provide peace of mind knowing that your affairs are in order and your loved ones will be taken care of according to your wishes.

Steps to Create an Estate Plan:

1.   Inventory Your Assets: Make a list of all your assets, including bank accounts, investments, real estate, and personal property.

2.   Identify Your Beneficiaries: Decide who you want to inherit your assets and how you want them to be distributed.

3.   Choose Your Executors and Trustees: Select trusted individuals to manage your estate and carry out your wishes.

4.   Create Your Estate Planning Documents: Work with an attorney to draft a will, trust, power of attorney, and healthcare directive that reflect your wishes and comply with state laws.

5.   Review and Update Your Plan Regularly: Review your estate plan periodically and update it as needed to reflect changes in your life, such as marriage, divorce, births, deaths, or changes in financial circumstances.

In conclusion, estate planning is an important part of financial planning that can help ensure your assets are distributed according to your wishes and provide for your loved ones after your death. By taking the time to create an estate plan, you can protect your legacy and provide for your family's future financial security.

Wills and Trusts: Understanding Your Estate Planning Options

Wills and trusts are two common estate planning tools that can help you manage and distribute your assets according to your wishes. While both serve similar purposes, they have different functions and can be used in different situations. Here's an overview of wills and trusts, including how they work and when to use them:

Wills:

1.   **Purpose**: A will is a legal document that outlines how you want your assets to be distributed after your death.

It can also appoint a guardian for any minor children and an executor to manage your estate.

2.   Key Features:

> Specifies who will inherit your assets and how they will be distributed.

> Allows you to name a guardian for minor children.

> Names an executor to carry out your wishes and manage your estate.

> Can be used to designate specific gifts or charitable donations.

3.   Benefits:

> Simple and cost-effective to create.

> Provides clear instructions for asset distribution.

> Can be easily updated to reflect changes in circumstances or preferences.

4.   Limitations:

> Subject to probate, which can be time-consuming and expensive.

> Does not offer privacy, as wills become public record once filed with the court.

> Does not provide for incapacity planning, as it only takes effect after your death.

Trusts:

1.   **Purpose**: A trust is a legal arrangement in which a trustee holds and manages assets for the benefit of a beneficiary. Trusts can be used to manage assets during your

lifetime, after your death, or for specific purposes, such as education or charitable giving.

2.   Key Features:

➢ Can be revocable or irrevocable, depending on your preferences.

➢ Allows you to specify how and when assets are distributed to beneficiaries.

➢ Can provide for incapacity planning by appointing a successor trustee to manage assets if you become incapacitated.

➢ Offers privacy, as trusts are not typically subject to probate and do not become public record.

3.   Benefits:

➢ Avoids probate, saving time and money.

➢ Provides flexibility in asset management and distribution.

➢ Can offer tax benefits, such as reducing estate taxes or capital gains taxes.

4.   Limitations:

➢ Can be more complex and expensive to create and maintain than a will.

➢ Requires transferring assets into the trust, which can be a logistical challenge.

➢ May not be necessary for smaller estates or those with simple distribution wishes.

Choosing Between a Will and a Trust:

The decision to use a will, a trust, or both depends on your individual circumstances and goals. In general, a will may be sufficient for smaller estates with straightforward distribution wishes, while a trust may be more appropriate for larger estates or those with specific needs, such as incapacity planning or privacy concerns.

Conclusion:

Wills and trusts are important estate planning tools that can help you ensure your assets are distributed according to your wishes. By understanding the differences between the two and how they can be used, you can make informed decisions about your estate plan and provide for your loved ones' future financial security.

Understanding Beneficiary Designations: Ensuring Your Assets Go to the Right People

Beneficiary designations are an important aspect of estate planning that allow you to specify who will receive your assets after your death. These designations are used for various types of accounts and assets, such as retirement accounts, life insurance policies, and bank accounts. Here's an overview of beneficiary designations, how they work, and why they are important:

How Beneficiary Designations Work:

1.   Definition: A beneficiary is the person or entity you designate to receive your assets upon your death.

2.   Types of Assets: Beneficiary designations are commonly used for retirement accounts (e.g., 401(k), IRA), life insurance policies, annuities, and some bank or investment accounts.

3.   Primary and Contingent Beneficiaries: You can name primary beneficiaries, who will receive the assets first, and contingent beneficiaries, who will receive the assets if the primary beneficiaries are deceased or unable to inherit.

4.   Updating Designations: It's important to review and update your beneficiary designations regularly, especially after major life events such as marriage, divorce, birth of a child, or death of a beneficiary.

Why Beneficiary Designations Are Important:

1.   Avoiding Probate: Assets with designated beneficiaries typically bypass the probate process, which can be time-consuming and expensive.

2.   Direct Transfer of Assets: Beneficiary designations allow for a direct transfer of assets to the designated beneficiaries, avoiding delays and potential disputes.

3.   Privacy: Beneficiary designations are private and do not become part of the public record, unlike assets distributed through a will, which is subject to probate.

4.   Tax Efficiency: Proper beneficiary designations can help minimize taxes on inherited assets, especially for retirement accounts.

Tips for Designating Beneficiaries:

1.   Be Specific: Provide full names, dates of birth, and contact information for your beneficiaries to ensure they can be easily located.

2.   Consider Contingent Beneficiaries: Designate contingent beneficiaries to ensure your assets are distributed according to your wishes if your primary beneficiaries are unable to inherit.

3. Review Regularly: Review your beneficiary designations regularly and update them as needed to reflect changes in your life circumstances or preferences.

4. Coordinate with Your Estate Plan: Ensure your beneficiary designations align with your overall estate plan, including your will and any trusts you have established.

In conclusion, beneficiary designations are an important aspect of estate planning that can help ensure your assets are distributed according to your wishes and provide for your loved ones' financial security. By understanding how beneficiary designations work and following best practices for designating beneficiaries, you can help ensure that your estate is settled smoothly and efficiently.

Minimizing Estate Taxes: Strategies for Preserving Your Wealth

Estate taxes, also known as inheritance taxes, can significantly reduce the amount of wealth passed on to your heirs. However, there are several strategies you can use to minimize estate taxes and preserve more of your assets for future generations. Here are some effective strategies:

1. Lifetime Gifts: One of the simplest ways to reduce your estate tax liability is to gift assets to your heirs during your lifetime. The IRS allows you to gift up to a certain amount each year (currently $15,000 per person) without incurring gift taxes. By gifting assets over time, you can reduce the size of your taxable estate.

2. Irrevocable Life Insurance Trust (ILIT): An ILIT is a trust that owns a life insurance policy on your life. Because the policy is owned by the trust, the death benefit is not included in your taxable estate. This can be an effective way to provide liquidity for estate taxes while minimizing the impact on your estate.

3. Qualified Personal Residence Trust (QPRT): A QPRT allows you to transfer ownership of your primary residence or vacation home to a trust for the benefit of your heirs while retaining the right to live in the property for a specified term. This can reduce the value of your taxable estate while allowing you to continue using the property.

4. Grantor Retained Annuity Trust (GRAT): A GRAT is a trust that allows you to transfer assets to your heirs while retaining an annuity payment for a specified term. At the end of the term, any remaining assets in the trust pass to your heirs free of gift and estate taxes. This can be an effective way to transfer appreciation on assets to your heirs tax-free.

5. Family Limited Partnership (FLP) or Limited Liability Company (LLC): Creating an FLP or LLC can allow you to transfer assets to your heirs at a discounted value, reducing the size of your taxable estate. By transferring ownership of assets to the partnership or LLC, you can also retain control over the assets during your lifetime.

6. Charitable Giving: Making charitable donations can reduce your taxable estate while supporting a cause you care about. Charitable donations are deductible from estate taxes, so they can be an effective way to reduce your estate tax liability while leaving a legacy of giving.

7. Qualified Terminable Interest Property (QTIP) Trust: A QTIP trust allows you to provide for a surviving spouse while ensuring that any remaining assets pass to your heirs free of estate taxes. This can be especially useful in blended families or situations where you want to provide for a surviving spouse but also ensure that assets ultimately pass to your children or other heirs.

8. Consult with an Estate Planning Professional: Estate planning can be complex, and the best strategies for minimizing estate taxes will depend on your individual circumstances. Consulting with an estate planning professional, such as an attorney or financial advisor, can help you develop a plan that meets your goals and minimizes your tax liability.

Lifestyle Considerations in Retirement:

Enhancing Your Quality of Life

Retirement is a significant life transition that often comes with a shift in priorities and lifestyle. Planning for retirement goes beyond financial considerations; it also involves thinking about how you want to live your life during this new chapter. Here are some lifestyle considerations to keep in mind as you plan for retirement:

1. Health and Wellness: Prioritizing your health and well-being is crucial in retirement. This includes maintaining a healthy diet, staying physically active, getting regular check-ups, and managing stress. Consider how you can incorporate health-promoting activities into your daily routine, such as exercise classes, outdoor activities, or hobbies that promote mental well-being.

2. Social Connections: Maintaining social connections and a sense of community is important for overall well-being in retirement. Consider joining clubs, volunteering, or participating in community activities to stay engaged and connected with others. Building and maintaining strong relationships with family and friends can also provide support and companionship in retirement.

3. Hobbies and Interests: Retirement is a great time to pursue hobbies and interests that you may not have had time for

during your working years. Whether it's painting, gardening, playing a musical instrument, or learning a new language, engaging in activities that bring you joy and fulfillment can enhance your retirement experience.

4. Travel and Adventure: Many retirees look forward to traveling and exploring new places in retirement. Whether it's a cross-country road trip, a European vacation, or a cruise around the world, travel can provide new experiences and create lasting memories. Consider how you can incorporate travel into your retirement plans, whether it's through long-term trips or shorter getaways.

5. Continued Learning: Retirement is a great time to continue learning and exploring new interests. Consider taking classes at a local community college or online, attending workshops or seminars, or joining a book club or discussion group. Lifelong learning can keep your mind sharp and engaged in retirement.

6. Housing Options: As you age, your housing needs may change. Consider whether your current home is suitable for aging in place or if you prefer downsizing to a smaller home or moving to a retirement community. Exploring different housing options can help you find a living arrangement that meets your needs and lifestyle preferences.

7. Financial Planning: While not strictly a lifestyle consideration, financial planning is essential for maintaining the lifestyle you desire in retirement. Consider working with a financial advisor to create a retirement budget, manage your retirement accounts, and ensure you have enough savings to support your lifestyle throughout retirement.

In Conclusion: Retirement is an opportunity to redefine how you live your life and prioritize what's most important to you. By considering these lifestyle factors, you can enhance your quality of life in retirement and create a fulfilling and meaningful retirement experience.

Choosing the Right Place to Live in Retirement

Deciding where to live in retirement is a significant decision that can impact your quality of life, finances, and overall well-being. Whether you choose to stay in your current home, downsize to a smaller residence, or relocate to a new area, it's important to consider several factors to ensure you make the right choice for your lifestyle and needs. Here are some key considerations when choosing where to live in retirement:

1. Cost of Living: Consider the cost of living in the area, including housing costs, property taxes, utilities, and everyday expenses such as groceries and healthcare. Choose a location where you can maintain your desired lifestyle within your budget.

2. Healthcare Access: Access to quality healthcare is crucial in retirement. Consider proximity to healthcare facilities, hospitals, and specialists, especially if you have ongoing medical needs or anticipate needing more healthcare services as you age.

3. Climate and Weather: Think about the climate and weather patterns of the area. Consider whether you prefer a mild climate, four seasons, or a warmer climate year-round. Climate can impact your comfort, health, and ability to enjoy outdoor activities.

4. Proximity to Family and Friends: Consider how close you want to be to family and friends. Living near loved ones can provide a support system and opportunities for socializing and caregiving, if needed.

5. Lifestyle and Amenities: Consider your preferred lifestyle and the amenities that are important to you. Whether you enjoy outdoor activities, cultural events, dining, or recreational opportunities, choose a location that offers the lifestyle you desire.

6. Housing Options: Evaluate housing options in the area, including single-family homes, condos, apartments, and retirement communities. Consider whether you want to age in place or downsize to a more manageable home.

7. Safety and Security: Choose a location that is safe and secure, with low crime rates and access to emergency services. Consider factors such as neighborhood safety, access to healthcare, and emergency preparedness.

8. Transportation and Accessibility: Consider transportation options in the area, including public transportation, access to major highways, and proximity to airports. Accessibility to amenities such as grocery stores, pharmacies, and recreational facilities is also important.

9. Community and Social Opportunities: Look for a community that offers social opportunities, such as clubs, classes, and activities, that align with your interests. Consider whether the community is age-friendly and offers support for retirees.

10. Tax Considerations: Research the tax implications of living in the area, including income taxes, property taxes, and sales taxes. Choose a location with tax policies that align with your financial goals.

In Conclusion: Choosing where to live in retirement is a personal decision that should take into account your lifestyle preferences, financial situation, and health needs. Consider these factors carefully to ensure you find a location that meets your needs and enhances your retirement experience.

Exploring Hobbies and Activities in Retirement: Enriching Your Golden Years

Retirement offers a unique opportunity to explore new hobbies, dive deeper into existing interests, and engage in activities that bring joy and fulfillment. Whether you're looking to stay active, connect with others, or simply enjoy your leisure time, there are countless hobbies and activities to consider in retirement. Here are some popular options to inspire you:

1. Outdoor Activities:

- Gardening: Cultivate a garden to grow flowers, vegetables, or herbs.

- Hiking: Explore nature trails, parks, and scenic areas.

- Birdwatching: Discover local bird species and their habitats.

- Fishing: Spend peaceful hours by the water, fishing for relaxation or sport.

2. Creative Pursuits:

- Painting or Drawing: Express yourself through visual art.

- Writing: Start a blog, pen a memoir, or write poetry.

- Crafts: Explore various crafts like knitting, crochet, woodworking, or pottery.

> Photography: Capture moments and scenes that inspire you.

3. Fitness and Wellness:

> Yoga or Tai Chi: Improve flexibility, balance, and mindfulness.

> Swimming: Enjoy a low-impact, full-body workout.

> Walking or Jogging: Stay active with regular walks or jogs.

> Dance: Join a dance class or group for fun and fitness.

4. Learning and Education:

> Art Classes: Take classes in painting, sculpture, or other art forms.

> Language Learning: Learn a new language or improve your language skills.

> Cooking or Baking: Enroll in cooking classes or experiment with new recipes.

> Music Lessons: Learn to play a musical instrument or join a choir.

5. Volunteering and Community Engagement:

> Mentoring: Share your skills and experience with others.

> Animal Shelters: Volunteer at a local animal shelter or rescue organization.

> Community Gardens: Get involved in community gardening projects.

> Charity Work: Volunteer for a cause you're passionate about.

6. Travel and Exploration:

> ➤ Road Trips: Explore new destinations by car, RV, or motorcycle.

> ➤ Cultural Tours: Visit museums, galleries, historical sites, and cultural events.

> ➤ Cruises: Enjoy leisurely travel and explore different destinations.

> ➤ Adventure Travel: Embark on adventurous trips like hiking, safaris, or wildlife tours.

7. Social and Leisure Activities:

> ➤ Book Clubs: Join a book club to discuss literature with others.

> ➤ Card Games: Play card games like bridge, poker, or canasta with friends.

> ➤ Golf or Tennis: Enjoy outdoor sports that promote social interaction.

> ➤ Dining Out: Explore local restaurants and cuisines with friends and family.

8. Technology and Digital Engagement:

> ➤ Social Media: Connect with friends and family online.

> ➤ Online Learning: Take advantage of online courses and workshops.

> ➤ Digital Photography: Learn digital photography techniques and editing.

In Conclusion:

Retirement is a time to pursue passions, discover new interests, and enjoy the freedom to engage in activities that bring you happiness and fulfillment. Whether you're interested in staying active, exploring your creative side, or giving back to your community, there's a wealth of hobbies and activities to explore in retirement. Embrace this exciting chapter of life and make the most of your golden years!

Travel and Leisure Planning in Retirement: Making the Most of Your Adventures

Retirement opens up a world of possibilities for travel and leisure, allowing you to explore new destinations, immerse yourself in different cultures, and create unforgettable memories. Whether you're dreaming of exotic adventures or leisurely escapes, careful planning can help you make the most of your travel experiences. Here's how to plan for travel and leisure in retirement:

> **Set Your Goals and Budget:**

> Determine your travel goals and priorities, whether it's visiting specific destinations, experiencing new cultures, or pursuing outdoor adventures.

> Establish a travel budget that considers your financial resources, including savings, pensions, and other income streams.

2. Choose Your Destinations:

> Research destinations that align with your interests and travel preferences, considering factors such as climate, attractions, safety, and accessibility.

> Create a travel bucket list and prioritize destinations based on your budget and travel goals.

3. Plan Your Itinerary:

> Develop a detailed travel itinerary that includes transportation, accommodations, activities, and meals.

> Consider factors such as travel time, rest days, and flexibility in your itinerary to ensure a balanced and enjoyable trip.

4. Consider Travel Insurance:

> Evaluate travel insurance options to protect yourself against unexpected events such as trip cancellations, medical emergencies, or lost luggage.

> Choose a policy that provides adequate coverage for your travel needs and destinations.

5. Prepare Your Documents:

> Ensure your passport is up-to-date and valid for at least six months beyond your travel dates.

> Check visa requirements for your destinations and apply for visas well in advance if necessary.

6. Pack Wisely:

> Pack light and bring versatile clothing and footwear suitable for different activities and weather conditions.

➢ Consider travel accessories such as travel-sized toiletries, a universal adapter, and a travel pillow for added comfort.

7. Stay Healthy and Safe:

➢ Visit your healthcare provider before traveling to ensure you are in good health and up-to-date on vaccinations.

➢ Research health and safety tips for your destinations, including any potential health risks or travel advisories.

8. Embrace Local Culture:

➢ Immerse yourself in the local culture by trying local cuisine, attending cultural events, and interacting with locals.

➢ Learn basic phrases in the local language to enhance your travel experience and show respect for the local culture.

9. Capture Memories:

➢ Document your travels through photos, videos, and journaling to preserve memories of your adventures.

➢ Create a travel scrapbook or digital album to share your experiences with friends and family.

10. Reflect and Rejuvenate:

➢ Take time to relax and rejuvenate during your travels, whether it's lounging on the beach, enjoying a spa day, or simply taking in the sights and sounds of a new destination.

> Reflect on your travel experiences and the memories you've created, and consider how they have enriched your life in retirement.

In Conclusion:

Travel and leisure in retirement offer endless opportunities for exploration, discovery, and personal growth. By carefully planning your travels and embracing new experiences, you can make the most of your retirement years and create lasting memories that will enrich your life for years to come.

Managing Risks in Retirement: Safeguarding Your Financial Future

Retirement is a time to enjoy the fruits of your labor and pursue your passions, but it also comes with financial risks that can impact your long-term security. By identifying and managing these risks, you can protect your retirement savings and enjoy peace of mind in your golden years. Here are some key risks to consider and strategies to manage them:

1. Longevity Risk:

Risk: Outliving your retirement savings due to increasing life expectancy.

Strategy: Plan for a longer retirement by estimating your life expectancy and factoring in inflation and healthcare costs. Consider annuities or other guaranteed income streams to provide lifetime income.

2. Market Risk:

Risk: Losses in investment values due to market fluctuations.

Strategy: Diversify your investment portfolio to reduce risk. Consider a mix of stocks, bonds, and other investments based on your risk tolerance and time horizon. Rebalance your portfolio regularly to maintain diversification.

3. Inflation Risk:

Risk: The erosion of purchasing power over time due to inflation.

Strategy: Invest in assets that can provide a hedge against inflation, such as inflation-protected bonds or stocks with a history of dividend growth. Consider adjusting your withdrawal rate for inflation to maintain your standard of living.

4. Healthcare Costs:

Risk: Rising healthcare costs, including long-term care expenses.

Strategy: Purchase long-term care insurance to cover potential costs. Consider a health savings account (HSA) to save for healthcare expenses in retirement. Stay healthy to reduce the risk of high medical bills.

5. Sequence of Returns Risk:

Risk: Experiencing poor investment returns early in retirement, which can deplete your savings.

Strategy: Consider a conservative withdrawal strategy or a bucket approach, where you maintain different portfolios for short-, medium-, and long-term needs. Have a cash reserve to cover expenses during market downturns.

6. Fraud and Scams:

Risk: Falling victim to financial fraud or scams.

Strategy: Be vigilant and skeptical of unsolicited offers or requests for money. Keep your personal and financial information secure. Consider working with a trusted financial advisor.

7. Social Security and Pension Risks:

Risk: Changes in Social Security benefits or pension plans.

Strategy: Understand your Social Security benefits and options. Consider delaying Social Security benefits to increase your monthly benefit. If you have a pension, understand the terms and ensure it is adequately funded.

8. Family and Caregiving Risks:

Risk: Providing financial support to family members or becoming a caregiver, which can impact your own financial well-being.

Strategy: Set clear boundaries and realistic expectations with family members. Consider long-term care insurance to help cover potential caregiving costs. Communicate your wishes and plans with your family.

In Conclusion:

Managing risks in retirement requires careful planning and a proactive approach. By identifying potential risks and implementing strategies to mitigate them, you can protect your financial future and enjoy a secure and fulfilling retirement.

Navigating Inflation and Purchasing Power Risk in Retirement

Inflation is the gradual increase in the price of goods and services over time, eroding the purchasing power of your money. For retirees, inflation poses a significant risk, as it can reduce the value of your savings and impact your standard of living. To protect against inflation and preserve your purchasing power in retirement, consider the following strategies:

1. Understand the Impact of Inflation:

> ➤ Inflation can erode the value of your savings over time, reducing your purchasing power.

> ➤ Even low inflation rates can have a significant impact on your retirement savings over a long retirement period.

2. Plan for Inflation:

> ➤ When creating a retirement budget, factor in inflation to ensure your income will keep pace with rising prices.

> ➤ Consider using a retirement calculator that accounts for inflation to estimate your future expenses and income needs.

3. Invest in Inflation-Protected Securities:

> ➤ Treasury Inflation-Protected Securities (TIPS) are bonds issued by the U.S. Treasury that are indexed to inflation.

> ➤ TIPS pay interest based on a fixed rate applied to the inflation-adjusted principal, providing a hedge against inflation.

4. Diversify Your Investment Portfolio:

> ➤ Invest in a diversified portfolio that includes assets that tend to perform well during inflationary periods, such as stocks, real estate, and commodities.

> ➤ Avoid holding too much cash or fixed-income investments that may not keep pace with inflation.

5. Consider Annuities:

> ➤ Annuities can provide a guaranteed income stream in retirement, which can help protect against inflation.

> ➤ Consider purchasing an inflation-adjusted annuity, which increases your payments over time to keep pace with inflation.

6. Monitor Your Spending:

> ➤ Keep track of your expenses and adjust your budget as needed to accommodate rising prices.

> ➤ Look for ways to reduce expenses or find more cost-effective alternatives to maintain your standard of living.

7. Stay Flexible:

> ➤ Be prepared to adjust your retirement plan as economic conditions change.

> ➤ Consider part-time work or other sources of income to supplement your retirement savings if needed.

8. Stay Informed:

> ➤ Stay informed about economic trends and inflation rates to make informed decisions about your investments and retirement planning.

> ➤ Consult with a financial advisor to discuss strategies for managing inflation risk in your retirement plan.

In Conclusion:

Inflation and purchasing power risk are important considerations for retirees. By understanding the impact of inflation, planning for it in your retirement budget, and implementing strategies to protect against it, you can help ensure that your savings will last throughout your retirement and maintain your standard of living.

Longevity Risk: Planning for a Longer Retirement

Longevity risk is the risk of outliving your retirement savings due to increasing life expectancy. As people live longer, they require more savings to support themselves in retirement. Managing longevity risk is crucial to ensure that you can maintain your desired lifestyle throughout your retirement years. Here are some strategies to help you plan for a longer retirement:

1. Estimate Your Life Expectancy:

> ➢ Use life expectancy calculators or consult with a financial advisor to estimate how long you may live.

> ➢ Consider factors such as your health, family history, and lifestyle when estimating your life expectancy.

2. Plan for a Longer Retirement:

> ➢ When planning for retirement, assume that you will live longer than the average life expectancy to account for longevity risk.

> ➢ Consider delaying retirement or working part-time in retirement to supplement your income and increase your savings.

3. Save More for Retirement:

> ➤ Save as much as possible for retirement to ensure you have enough savings to last throughout your retirement years.

> ➤ Take advantage of retirement accounts such as 401(k) s, IRAs, and other tax-advantaged savings vehicles to maximize your savings.

4. Invest for the Long Term:

> ➤ Invest in a diversified portfolio that includes a mix of stocks, bonds, and other assets suited to your risk tolerance and time horizon.

> ➤ Consider consulting with a financial advisor to develop an investment strategy that addresses longevity risk.

5. Purchase Annuities or Longevity Insurance:

> ➤ Annuities and longevity insurance can provide a guaranteed income stream that lasts for life, helping to protect against longevity risk.

> ➤ Consider purchasing an annuity with inflation protection to ensure that your income keeps pace with rising prices.

6. Consider Health Care Costs:

> ➤ Plan for potential increases in health care costs as you age, including long-term care expenses.

> ➤ Consider purchasing long-term care insurance to help cover these costs and protect your savings.

7. Stay Healthy:

> ➢ Maintaining a healthy lifestyle can help reduce the risk of health issues that could impact your longevity and increase your medical expenses.

> ➢ Eat a balanced diet, exercise regularly, get regular check-ups, and avoid unhealthy habits such as smoking.

8. Stay Informed and Adjust Your Plan:

> ➢ Stay informed about economic trends, changes in life expectancy, and other factors that could impact your retirement plan.

> ➢ Periodically review your retirement plan and make adjustments as needed to ensure it remains on track to meet your goals.

In Conclusion:

Longevity risk is a significant consideration in retirement planning. By estimating your life expectancy, saving more for retirement, investing wisely, considering insurance options, planning for health care costs, and staying informed, you can manage longevity risk and enjoy a financially secure retirement.

Navigating Market Risk and Economic Downturns in Retirement

Market risk and economic downturns can have a significant impact on your retirement savings and income. It's important to understand these risks and implement strategies to protect your financial well-being in retirement. Here are some key considerations:

1. Understand Market Risk:

➢ Market risk refers to the potential for investment losses due to market fluctuations.

➢ Stocks and other equity investments are more volatile and carry higher market risk compared to bonds and cash equivalents.

2. Diversify Your Portfolio:

➢ Diversification is key to managing market risk. Spread your investments across different asset classes (stocks, bonds, real estate) to reduce the impact of a downturn in any one sector.

➢ Consider rebalancing your portfolio regularly to maintain your desired asset allocation.

3. Stay Invested for the Long Term:

➢ While market downturns can be unsettling, it's important to stay invested for the long term.

➢ Historically, markets have recovered from downturns, and long-term investors have been rewarded for staying the course.

4. Have a Cash Reserve:

➢ Maintain an emergency fund or cash reserve to cover expenses in case of a market downturn or other unexpected financial need.

➢ Having a cash cushion can help you avoid selling investments at a loss during a market downturn.

5. Consider Guaranteed Income Sources:

- ➢ Consider purchasing annuities or other guaranteed income products to provide a steady income stream in retirement.

- ➢ Guaranteed income sources can help protect against market risk and provide peace of mind in retirement.

6. Monitor Your Investments:

- ➢ Stay informed about market trends and economic indicators that could impact your investments.

- ➢ Consider working with a financial advisor to help you make informed decisions about your investments.

7. Adjust Your Withdrawal Rate:

- ➢ During a market downturn, consider reducing your withdrawal rate from your retirement savings to preserve your nest egg.

- ➢ A lower withdrawal rate can help your savings last longer during periods of market volatility.

8. Stay Flexible:

- ➢ Be prepared to adjust your retirement plan in response to changing market conditions.

- ➢ Consider part-time work or other sources of income to supplement your retirement savings during a market downturn.

9. Stay Calm and Avoid Emotional Decisions:

> ➢ Market downturns can be stressful, but it's important to avoid making hasty decisions based on fear or panic.

> ➢ Stick to your long-term investment plan and avoid trying to time the market.

In Conclusion:

Market risk and economic downturns are inherent risks in retirement investing. By understanding these risks, diversifying your portfolio, staying invested for the long term, and having a plan in place to manage downturns, you can help protect your retirement savings and achieve your financial goals in retirement.

Preparing for Unexpected Events

Retirement is a time to enjoy the fruits of your labor and pursue your passions, but it's also important to be prepared for unexpected events that can impact your financial security. By planning ahead and taking steps to protect yourself against unforeseen circumstances, you can help ensure a more secure retirement. Here are some key considerations:

1. Emergency Fund:

> ➤ Maintain an emergency fund to cover unexpected expenses, such as medical bills or home repairs.

> ➤ Aim to have enough savings to cover three to six months' worth of living expenses.

2. Health Care Costs:

> ➤ Health care expenses can be a major financial burden in retirement.

> ➤ Consider purchasing long-term care insurance to help cover the costs of nursing home care or home health care.

3. Insurance Coverage:

> ➤ Review your insurance coverage, including health, life, and property insurance, to ensure you have adequate protection.

> Consider umbrella insurance to provide additional liability coverage beyond your standard policies.

4. Estate Planning:

> Create or update your estate plan to ensure your assets are distributed according to your wishes.

> Consider establishing a trust to help avoid probate and provide for your heirs in a tax-efficient manner.

5. Longevity Risk:

> Plan for a longer retirement by estimating your life expectancy and factoring in inflation and health care costs.

> Consider purchasing an annuity or other guaranteed income product to provide a steady income stream for life.

6. Market Volatility:

> Diversify your investment portfolio to reduce the impact of market volatility.

> Consider working with a financial advisor to develop an investment strategy that aligns with your risk tolerance and financial goals.

7. Legal Documents:

> Prepare or update legal documents, such as a will, power of attorney, and advance directive, to ensure your wishes are carried out in the event of incapacity or death.

> ➤ Consider appointing a trusted individual to make financial and medical decisions on your behalf if you are unable to do so.

8. Stay Informed:

> ➤ Stay informed about economic trends, tax law changes, and other factors that could impact your financial situation.

> ➤ Consider attending financial planning workshops or seminars to learn more about retirement planning and investment strategies.

9. Stay Flexible:

> ➤ Be prepared to adjust your retirement plan in response to changing circumstances.

> ➤ Consider working part-time or reducing expenses during times of financial uncertainty.

In Conclusion:

Preparing for unexpected events in retirement requires careful planning and foresight. By establishing an emergency fund, managing health care costs, maintaining adequate insurance coverage, and staying informed about financial matters, you can help protect your financial security and enjoy a more secure retirement.

Emergency Funds in Retirement: Building a Financial Safety Net

In retirement, having an emergency fund is just as important as it is during your working years, if not more so. Unexpected expenses can arise at any time, and having a financial safety net can help you avoid dipping into your retirement savings prematurely. Here's how to build and maintain an emergency fund in retirement:

1. Determine Your Emergency Fund Needs:

➤ Aim to save enough to cover three to six months' worth of living expenses.

➤ Consider your current expenses, including housing, utilities, groceries, and healthcare costs, when determining your emergency fund target.

2. Build Your Emergency Fund:

➤ Set a savings goal and contribute regularly to your emergency fund.

➤ Consider automating your savings by setting up automatic transfers from your checking account to your emergency fund.

3. Keep Your Emergency Fund Separate:

➤ Keep your emergency fund in a separate savings account from your regular checking and savings accounts.

➤ This can help prevent you from using the funds for non-emergencies and ensure they are readily accessible when needed.

4. Use Your Emergency Fund Wisely:

➤ Only use your emergency fund for true emergencies, such as unexpected medical bills or home repairs.

➢ Avoid using your emergency fund for discretionary expenses or non-urgent purchases.

5. Replenish Your Emergency Fund:

➢ If you need to use funds from your emergency fund, make it a priority to replenish them as soon as possible.

➢ Adjust your budget if necessary to increase your savings rate until your emergency fund is fully replenished.

6. Review and Adjust Regularly:

➢ Regularly review your emergency fund needs and adjust your savings goals as needed.

➢ Consider increasing your emergency fund if your expenses or circumstances change.

7. Consider Other Sources of Emergency Funds:

➢ In addition to your emergency fund, consider other sources of funds in case of emergencies, such as a home equity line of credit (HELOC) or a Roth IRA (withdrawing contributions, not earnings).

8. Financial Planning:

➢ Include your emergency fund in your overall financial plan and retirement strategy.

➢ Work with a financial advisor to ensure your emergency fund is adequate and aligned with your financial goals.

In Conclusion:

Having an emergency fund in retirement is essential for financial security and peace of mind. By setting aside funds for unexpected expenses, you can protect your retirement savings and avoid financial hardship in times of need. Start building your emergency fund today to prepare for whatever the future may bring.

Managing Major Expenses in Retirement: A Strategic Approach

Retirement often brings a fixed income, making it crucial to manage major expenses wisely to avoid financial strain. Whether it's healthcare costs, home repairs, or other significant expenditures, planning ahead can help you navigate these expenses with greater ease. Here's how to deal with major expenses in retirement:

1. Healthcare Costs:

> ➢ Health Insurance: Ensure you have comprehensive health insurance coverage, including Medicare and supplemental insurance if needed.

> ➢ Long-Term Care Insurance: Consider purchasing long-term care insurance to help cover potential costs associated with nursing home care or in-home assistance.

> ➢ Health Savings Account (HSA): Contribute to an HSA if you have a high-deductible health plan to save for future medical expenses tax-free.

2. Home Repairs and Maintenance:

➢ Budget for Maintenance: Set aside funds in your budget for regular home maintenance to prevent costly repairs down the line.

➢ Emergency Fund: Maintain an emergency fund specifically for home repairs and unexpected expenses.

3. Vehicle Expenses:

➢ Budget for Maintenance: Include vehicle maintenance and repairs in your budget to avoid unexpected expenses.

➢ Consider Transportation Alternatives: Evaluate whether you need a car in retirement or if you can rely on public transportation, ridesharing, or other alternatives.

4. Travel and Leisure:

➢ Plan Ahead: Budget for travel and leisure activities and plan your trips during off-peak times to save money.

➢ Travel Insurance: Consider purchasing travel insurance to protect against unexpected trip cancellations or medical emergencies.

5. Family Support:

➢ Set Boundaries: Establish clear boundaries with family members regarding financial support to avoid straining your own finances.

> Financial Planning: Include potential family support in your overall financial plan to ensure it aligns with your retirement goals.

6. Home Modifications:

> Aging in Place: Consider making home modifications to allow you to age in place safely and comfortably.

> Cost-Effective Solutions: Explore cost-effective solutions for home modifications, such as installing grab bars or ramps.

7. Legal and Estate Planning:

> Consult Professionals: Seek advice from legal and financial professionals to ensure your estate plan is comprehensive and protects your assets.

> Power of Attorney: Consider establishing a power of attorney to manage your affairs if you become incapacitated.

8. Consider Financing Options:

> Home Equity: Use a home equity line of credit (HELOC) or reverse mortgage to fund major expenses if needed.

> Personal Loans: Explore personal loans as a financing option for major expenses, but be mindful of interest rates and repayment terms.

In Conclusion:

Dealing with major expenses in retirement requires careful planning and consideration. By budgeting for these expenses, exploring financing options, and making informed decisions, you can manage major expenses effectively and protect your financial well-being in retirement.

Monitoring and Adjusting Your Retirement Plan:

Staying on Track for Financial Security

Retirement planning is not a one-time task; it requires ongoing monitoring and adjustments to ensure you stay on track to meet your financial goals. Regularly reviewing your retirement plan can help you identify potential issues early and make necessary changes to maximize your savings and income in retirement. Here's how to effectively monitor and adjust your retirement plan:

1. Review Your Financial Goals:

➢ Regularly revisit your retirement goals and assess whether they are still realistic and achievable.

➢ Consider any changes in your life circumstances or financial situation that may impact your goals.

2. Evaluate Your Investment Portfolio:

➢ Review your investment portfolio regularly to ensure it aligns with your risk tolerance and financial goals.

➢ Consider rebalancing your portfolio periodically to maintain your desired asset allocation.

3. Assess Your Retirement Income:

> ➢ Estimate your retirement income from various sources, including Social Security, pensions, and retirement accounts.

> ➢ Evaluate whether your projected income is sufficient to cover your expenses in retirement.

4. Monitor Your Expenses:

> ➢ Keep track of your expenses in retirement and compare them to your budget.

> ➢ Identify any areas where you may be overspending or where you can reduce expenses.

5. Consider Inflation and Rising Costs:

> ➢ Account for inflation and rising costs when planning for retirement expenses.

> ➢ Adjust your retirement plan periodically to ensure your savings and income keep pace with inflation.

6. Plan for Healthcare Costs:

> ➢ Review your healthcare needs and expenses regularly and adjust your retirement plan accordingly.

> ➢ Consider purchasing long-term care insurance to help cover potential future healthcare costs.

7. Stay Informed About Tax Laws:

> ➢ Stay informed about changes in tax laws that may impact your retirement savings and income.

> ➤ Consider consulting with a tax advisor to optimize your retirement tax strategy.

8. Be Prepared for Market Volatility:

> ➤ Monitor market trends and economic indicators that may impact your investments.

> ➤ Be prepared to adjust your investment strategy in response to market volatility.

9. Seek Professional Advice:

> ➤ Consider working with a financial advisor to help you monitor and adjust your retirement plan.

> ➤ A financial advisor can provide personalized advice and recommendations based on your individual financial situation and goals.

10. Stay Flexible and Open to Adjustments:

> ➤ Be willing to make adjustments to your retirement plan as needed based on changing circumstances.

> ➤ Remain flexible and open to new strategies that can help you achieve your retirement goals.

In Conclusion:

Monitoring and adjusting your retirement plan regularly is essential to staying on track for financial security in retirement. By regularly reviewing your goals, evaluating your investment portfolio and retirement income, monitoring your expenses, and staying informed about relevant financial and tax issues, you can make informed decisions that will help you achieve a financially secure retirement.

How to Regularly Review Your Retirement Plan for Financial Success

Regularly reviewing your retirement plan is crucial to ensure that you stay on track to meet your financial goals. By assessing your progress and making adjustments as needed, you can enhance your financial security and make the most of your retirement years. Here's a step-by-step guide on how to regularly review your retirement plan:

1. Set a Review Schedule:

➤ Establish a regular schedule for reviewing your retirement plan, such as quarterly, semi-annually, or annually.

➤ Mark your review dates on your calendar to ensure you don't overlook them.

2. Gather Your Financial Documents:

➤ Collect all relevant financial documents, including bank statements, investment account statements, retirement account statements, and any other financial records.

3. Review Your Financial Goals:

➤ Revisit your retirement goals and assess whether they are still realistic and achievable.

➤ Consider any changes in your life circumstances or financial situation that may impact your goals.

4. Evaluate Your Investment Portfolio:

➤ Review your investment portfolio to ensure it aligns with your risk tolerance and financial goals.

> Consider rebalancing your portfolio if necessary to maintain your desired asset allocation.

5. Assess Your Retirement Income:

> Estimate your retirement income from various sources, including Social Security, pensions, and retirement accounts.

> Evaluate whether your projected income is sufficient to cover your expenses in retirement.

6. Monitor Your Expenses:

> Keep track of your expenses in retirement and compare them to your budget.

> Identify any areas where you may be overspending or where you can reduce expenses.

7. Consider Inflation and Rising Costs:

> Account for inflation and rising costs when planning for retirement expenses.

> Adjust your retirement plan periodically to ensure your savings and income keep pace with inflation.

8. Plan for Healthcare Costs:

> Review your healthcare needs and expenses regularly and adjust your retirement plan accordingly.

> Consider purchasing long-term care insurance to help cover potential future healthcare costs.

9. Stay Informed About Tax Laws:

➢ Stay informed about changes in tax laws that may impact your retirement savings and income.

➢ Consider consulting with a tax advisor to optimize your retirement tax strategy.

10. Be Prepared for Market Volatility:

➢ Monitor market trends and economic indicators that may impact your investments.

➢ Be prepared to adjust your investment strategy in response to market volatility.

11. Seek Professional Advice:

➢ Consider working with a financial advisor to help you review and adjust your retirement plan.

➢ A financial advisor can provide personalized advice and recommendations based on your individual financial situation and goals.

12. Stay Flexible and Open to Adjustments:

➢ Be willing to make adjustments to your retirement plan as needed based on changing circumstances.

➢ Remain flexible and open to new strategies that can help you achieve your retirement goals.

13. Document Your Review Process:

➢ Keep a record of your review process, including any changes you make to your retirement plan.

> This documentation can help you track your progress over time and make more informed decisions in the future.

In Conclusion:

Regularly reviewing your retirement plan is essential to ensure that you stay on track for financial success in retirement. By following these steps and staying proactive about managing your finances, you can enhance your financial security and enjoy a more comfortable retirement.

Making Adjustments to Your Retirement Plan Based on Changing Circumstances

Life is full of surprises, and as you move through retirement, your circumstances may change. Whether it's a shift in your health, family dynamics, or financial situation, being able to adjust your retirement plan accordingly is key to maintaining financial stability. Here's how to make adjustments based on changing circumstances:

1. Health Changes:

> If your health deteriorates, reassess your healthcare needs and expenses.

> Consider how changes in your health may impact your retirement budget and long-term care plans.

2. Family Changes:

> If you experience a change in family status, such as a marriage, divorce, birth, or death in the family, review your financial obligations and goals.

> Update your beneficiary designations and estate plan to reflect any changes in your family situation.

3. Financial Changes:

> ➤ If your income or expenses change, adjust your retirement budget accordingly.

> ➤ Consider whether you need to increase or decrease your retirement savings contributions based on your financial situation.

4. Market Conditions:

> ➤ Monitor market trends and economic indicators that may impact your investments.

> ➤ Adjust your investment strategy if market conditions warrant a change to protect your retirement savings.

5. Tax Law Changes:

> ➤ Stay informed about changes in tax laws that may impact your retirement savings and income.

> ➤ Adjust your tax planning strategies as needed to minimize your tax burden in retirement.

6. Longevity Considerations:

> ➤ If you live longer than expected, reassess your retirement income needs and adjust your withdrawal strategy.

> ➤ Consider purchasing annuities or other income products to provide a guaranteed income stream for life.

7. Housing Considerations:

➢ If your housing needs change, such as downsizing or relocating, reassess your housing expenses and budget.

➢ Consider how changes in your housing situation may impact your overall retirement plan.

8. Legal and Estate Planning:

➢ Review your legal documents, such as your will, power of attorney, and advance directive, to ensure they reflect your current wishes.

➢ Consider updating your estate plan to account for any changes in your financial or family situation.

9. Professional Advice:

➢ Consult with a financial advisor or tax professional to help you make informed decisions about adjusting your retirement plan.

➢ A professional can provide personalized advice based on your individual circumstances and financial goals.

10. Stay Flexible:

➢ Be open to making adjustments to your retirement plan as needed to adapt to changing circumstances.

➢ Remain flexible and willing to explore new strategies to help you achieve your retirement goals.

In Conclusion:

Being able to adjust your retirement plan based on changing circumstances is essential to maintaining financial stability in retirement. By staying proactive and regularly reviewing your plan, you can adapt to life's changes and ensure that your retirement remains secure and comfortable.

Conclusion:

Enjoying a Secure and Fulfilling Retirement

Retirement is a time of new beginnings, a chapter in life where you can enjoy the fruits of your labor and pursue your passions. It's a time to relax, explore new interests, and spend quality time with loved ones. However, to truly enjoy a secure and fulfilling retirement, careful planning and preparation are essential. This book has provided a comprehensive guide to help you navigate the complexities of retirement planning, from setting goals and creating a budget to managing investments and preparing for unexpected events.

Reflecting on the Journey:

As you reflect on the journey of planning for retirement, remember that it's not just about the destination but the path you take to get there. Each decision you make along the way, from saving diligently to investing wisely, contributes to the overall success of your retirement plan. By taking the time to educate yourself and make informed decisions, you are setting yourself up for a more secure and fulfilling retirement.

Setting the Foundation:

At the heart of a successful retirement plan is a solid foundation built on clear goals and a realistic assessment of your financial situation. By setting specific, measurable, achievable, relevant, and time-bound (SMART) goals, you can create a roadmap that guides your financial decisions and keeps you on track toward a secure retirement.

Managing Your Finances:

Managing your finances in retirement requires careful attention to detail and a proactive approach. From creating a retirement budget to monitoring your expenses and adjusting your plan as needed, staying on top of your finances is key to enjoying a secure retirement.

Investing for the Future:

Investing wisely is crucial to building wealth and achieving your long-term financial goals. By diversifying your investment portfolio, staying informed about market trends, and seeking professional advice when needed, you can make the most of your investments and maximize your retirement savings.

Preparing for the Unexpected:

Life is unpredictable, and preparing for the unexpected is an important part of retirement planning. By having an emergency fund, adequate insurance coverage, and a plan for managing major expenses, you can protect yourself against financial setbacks and enjoy greater peace of mind in retirement.

Embracing the Lifestyle:

Retirement is not just about financial security; it's also about embracing a lifestyle that brings you joy and fulfillment. Whether it's pursuing hobbies and interests, traveling, or spending time with family and friends, retirement is your time to do the things you love and create memories that will last a lifetime.

Looking Ahead:

As you embark on this new chapter of your life, remember that retirement is not the end of the road but a new beginning. By staying proactive, staying informed, and staying flexible, you can enjoy a secure and fulfilling retirement that allows you to live life to the fullest.

In Conclusion:

Enjoying a secure and fulfilling retirement is within reach for anyone willing to put in the time and effort to plan for it. By following the advice in this book and taking control of your financial future, you can enjoy a retirement that is not only financially secure but also personally fulfilling. So, here's to a happy and prosperous retirement—may it be everything you've dreamed of and more!